THE ROMANCE OF THE MARTIN CONNOR

ON THE AMAZON

THE ROMANCE OF
THE MARTIN CONNOR

BY

OSWALD KENDALL

BOSTON AND NEW YORK
HOUGHTON MIFFLIN COMPANY
The Riverside Press Cambridge
1916

CONTENTS

I. Introduces some People and a Ship . . . 1

II. Departure 27

III. A Test for Ship and Seamanship 51

IV. A Different World 71

V. Up the Amazon 96

VI. Trouble 124

VII. The Complete Anglers 144

VIII. The Blowgun Indians 168

IX. In which the Martin Connor retreats strate-
gically 192

X. A Voice from the Darkness 217

XI. The Great Discovery 240

XII. Disappearance of Captain Hawks 259

XIII. A Raid by Night 287

XIV. Two and Three Quarters Millions in Gold . . 309

ILLUSTRATIONS

ON THE AMAZON . . *Colored Frontispiece by Will Hammell*

THE ALLIGATOR WAS IN THE AIR (page 158) . . *Title-Page*

"'ERE, MISTER MATE, WHERE'S THIS SEA COMIN' FROM?"   46

A YELL CAME FROM THE GALLEY 58

"D' YO' WANT TO DIE RIGHT OFF?" 74

"YOU DID IT TO SAVE MY LIFE". 138

HE RAN HIM WITH GREAT SPEED INTO THE LAMP LOCKER . 192

HE BLEW A SHARP BREATH INTO THE GUN 262

THE WATER GREW ROUGHER 282

*With the exception of the frontispiece
the illustrations are by George Varian*

THE ROMANCE OF
THE MARTIN CONNOR

CHAPTER I

INTRODUCES SOME PEOPLE AND A SHIP

As I finished winding the chronometers, Captain
Matthew Hawks entered the charthouse of the
Martin Connor and slapped some papers down
upon the desk.

"I'm through with the whole bunch," said he
with a restrained emphasis that marked an endeavour to keep his temper, as he glared at me
with keen, cold, grey eyes. "I tell you, Grummet, I'm through with the whole bunch!" —
and he hit the pile of papers a smack with his
open hand.

I glanced down to see if he had cracked the top
of the desk and said: "Yes, sir," sympathetically.

"I want coal," continued my commander.

"Yes, sir, certainly."

"Coal in bunkers, Grummet, and coal in number two hold."

"Yes, sir. Are you going to —"

"Yes, I am!" he replied. "I'm going to start

right now. Just as soon as I can get under weigh.
I'll wait no longer. I'll fool around no longer.
And I'll spend no more good money in graft."

"What's the fresh trouble, sir?" I inquired.

"Ever hear of the Rio Maranon Rubber Company, Grummet?"

"There has been a good deal about 'em in the
papers, lately, sir, and some one has written a
book in which he calls them some very hard
names."

"He has my sympathy, though he could n't
call 'em any harder names than I have. I scared
their representative, anyway. I scared him stiff.
He came to see me here in Galveston."

I grinned, for my commander was a large man
with a large-featured, sunburned face, capable of
scaring a good many people if he did but try. In
fact, I have seen him scare a whole ship's crew
into semi-hysteria more than once, and I considered it likely that the agent for the Rio
Maranon Rubber Company had been through a
pretty bad time.

"Was he a Dago, sir?" I asked.

"No, American, from New York. One of these
smart business men with nose-glasses and pretty
finger-nails. I made him jump. I kept him jumping. Grummet, he's jumping now! He came
down here thinking I was just a Westerner, a
Californian, the captain of a small cargo tramp.

So I am. But I'm not the kind he thought I was. I pretty near made him cry! I told him that the company he represented had got eighteen hundred dollars out of me all for nothing, and I was careful to explain to him that what money I had I have made for myself. I was quiet enough at first and I let him talk. Always open negotiations by making the other man talk, Grummet."

"Yes, sir."

"He threw dollars and technicalities at me, and tried to be kind to me and explain what he meant, because I am only a shipmaster and could not be expected to know all the rank rotten inside workings of stock markets and finance generally. When he had finished I had my say. I said: 'Look you here, Mr. Man, your company is a company of rogues, robbers, and thieves, and you are a fit representative for such a crowd.'"

"Did you open up on him that way, sir?" I asked.

"I did, Grummet; that's when he started to jump! I asked him in several different ways why the Rio Maranon Company had first granted me a concession to trade in the Upper Amazon country and had then withdrawn the concession. I asked him why the reports from my partner, Colonel Ezra Calvin, who is on the spot, had been stopped for the last six months. And then I asked him plumb out what the Rio Maranon had done to or with Ezra, and he could n't or would n't say a thing. He just put me off with a stream of words! Say! Grummet! These business men sure can talk and say nothing! So I said [here my commander hit the charthouse desk another ringing blow]: 'Quit making that noise and listen to me! When I applied to the Government of Peru and the Government of Colombia for a trading concession, they referred me to your company. When I applied to your company, they referred me back to the Governments of Peru and Colombia; and so it went on for months, during which time I have spent, in all, eighteen hundred good American dollars for — what! I get my concession, finally. In consequence I buy my trade goods — more money spent — and then when all is ready you withdraw your concession! Now, I don't mind the money, — I can stick that, — and I don't so much fret over all the bother. But what does trouble me is this silence of my partner, Colonel Ezra Calvin.' Then, after a lot more talk (I was doing the talking then), I explained just what I was going to do, for I have no intention of going round behind 'em, or of playin' 'em any mean tricks whatever they may have done to me. I told him — that business man with the nose-glasses — that I had, already, a charter from the Rio Maloca Rubber Company (which company, I guess, is just about owned by the Rio Maranon people) for the due conveyance of certain goods to their up-river headquarters. I explained that I was going to carry that out as an ordinary matter of business. But afterwards, — and I made this clear to him, — afterwards I intended to hunt for and find my partner, Colonel Ezra Calvin, and when I had found him I intended trading upon my own account."

"Was it well to say that, sir?" I asked.

"Why not, Grummet? Snakes alive! Am I an infant that needs a nursemaid? Are you and the rest of the crowd on this ship infants? They can't eat us, can they? This is an American ship, ain't it? There's an American flag at her stern, is n't there? Well, what they goin' to do, — eh?"

"It's a long way from home, up that river, sir."

"It sure is. But what's that got to do with it? I guess you and I have been a long way from home before, Grummet, you and I and that little man in the galley. Theoretically, I should go to Washington, and I should say: 'Please, who owns this up-river country anyway? Is it Peru? Is it Colombia? Is it Ecuador? Is it Brazil? Or is it this Rio Maranon Company? For there's a patch of land up there about the size of Texas that every one claims and which nobody rules,

and there ain't a man living that I can find who
knows where the frontier is.' Then Washington
would get busy, and in about ten years I'd hear
all about it. Meanwhile, what's to become of my
partner in the deal? He went prospecting for
trade up the Amazon River eighteen months
ago, and at first I got his reports regularly
enough, considering the difficulties. Wherever
he went he met with opposition and trouble arranged by this Rio Maranon Company, while the
last two letters I had from him warned me that
he was liable to find himself at any moment in a
really serious fix. As they have already robbed
him of his goods and threatened his life, the serious fix he speaks of must mean something!"

"And you have n't heard from him for six
months, sir?"

"Not a word, Grummet."

"What kind of a man is he, sir?"

"A piece of New England granite with all the
hard corners left sticking out for the wrong kind
of man to bump up against. Except that he is a
landsman he's a regular Down-Easter of the old
sailing-packet type — not one of these soft modern business men with nose-glasses that live in
a cage near the sky and get round-shouldered
shouting through a 'phone all day and half the
night! You'd like Calvin. He's what Wilfred
would call a 'little bit of All-Right.' Not that

he's small. He's several yards high, in fact, and he's got a voice on him like the sirens at Cape Race."

"And you think that he has fallen against this rubber trust and that they have bottled him, sir?"

"Looks like it to me. Moreover, that part of the world is less explored than the middle of Africa, and where we are going is some hundreds of miles beyond. I have been busy learning, but I can't learn much. The latest maps print 'La Montana' over a stretch the size of the Western States, and to fill in the gaps the geographers throw in a river or two the size of the St. Lawrence, — rivers which may or may not be there. The main Amazon stream is all right, so is the main Negro, Madeira, Yapura, and Putumayo, and so on. The tributary streams, however, are a different story; they are just wherever you like to put them, and it's up a tributary of a tributary that we are bound."

Captain Hawks paused and drummed his fingers upon the desk before him, looking out through the heavy plate-glass charthouse windows down upon the sun-bathed main deck of the *Martin Connor*. A great silence filled the empty ship "asleep upon her iron," a silence hardly broken by the soft humming of the trade wind in the funnel stays and wire rigging of our stumpy masts. A smell of boiling ham floated upwards from the galley, and very occasionally came the voice of our cook raised in song.

"The fact," continued Captain Hawks, "that I have here this *bona-fide* contract with the Rio Maloca Rubber Company to carry goods to their up-river headquarters, which are within a few hundred miles of where I want to go; and the fact that, though I am willing to pay for a concession, it is neither refused in an official manner nor granted because I am butting into the Rio Maranon rubber trust, have decided me to go ahead and do my trading and pay for my concession afterwards — since they won't let me pay for it now."

"Meanwhile they will drop upon us as poachers, sir."

"Grummet, don't croak. When I had that contract with the Liverpool firm, and we did sixteen trips across the Atlantic up and down Watery Lane, you were as sick of it as I was. You likened us to the Cunard! Well, Mr. Mate, some years ago, before I went into steam, you and I and Cert'nly Wilfred in the Galley, mighty near froze to death in the Arctic.[1] We are now going to be baked and boiled and stewed to death by way of a change."

"Yes, sir."

[1] See *Captain Protheroe's Fortune.* A. C. McClurg & Co., Chicago.

"Nothing like variety, Grummet."

"No, sir. What's the cargo for this Rio Maloca Rubber Company?"

"Portable buildings, firearms, ammunition, groceries, drugs, wines and spirits, machetes, chemicals, sewing machines, and a variety of oddments for the resident manager and his friends. The resident manager is a German, Eichholz by name, and we shall pick up a director of the company at Para, a Dago with the adopted English name of — now, listen, Grummet — Alonzo Makepeace Massingbird."

"Thunder and lightning!" I exclaimed.

"Just so. The rest of the cargo will be similar in character and will include phonographs, looking-glasses, and articles of adornment for the person calculated to make the wearer both proud and happy. These last are for my own private trading, which trading, Grummet, need not be published in the newspapers."

I nodded.

"Meanwhile — coal, Mr. Mate; coal in bunkers and coal in number two hold."

I stepped out on to the bridge-deck to issue my orders, leaving Captain Hawks to lock away his papers in the ship's safe. To north and westward, blue in the distance, was the row of piles marking the Government Ship Channel, and on the left, the beacon on Edward Point, while all about us stretched the vast bay of Galveston shimmering in the early morning light. I ran down the ladder and sought our chief engineer, a large-boned Scotchman named Andrew Kinnaird McLushley, a man who possessed a supreme knowledge of reciprocating machinery, a bitter and sardonic humour, a red-rimmed fighting eye, and a passion for the poetry of Mrs. Felicia Hemans. I found him seated in an oil-stained canvas deck-chair cleaning out a black-looking briar pipe that had seen much service.

"Have you any steam, Mr. McLushley?" I asked.

"I have an' I have not, Mr. Grummet," replied the Scotchman with all the caution that marked his most trivial utterance; "there's plenty in the winches for the last twa days, awaitin' ye'r orrd'rs that did not come."

"We are going inshore to coal," said I.

"Then I'll have ye enough to move her wi' inside the hour." And he rose stiffly, removed his steel-rimmed spectacles from his battered nose, pocketed his pipe, and clattered down into the warm, echoing deeps of the ship, where I heard his harsh, rasping voice calling his second and his third assistants.

Captain Hawks returned ashore in a launch, leaving the ship to me. I got our temporary crew to work laying out wire hawsers, and in less than an hour Mr. McLushley whistled up the bridge-tube and delivered the concise and cryptic message: "Can do."

"Thank you, Mr. McLushley," I replied, and replaced the whistle. "Mr. Hanks," I continued, to our young New England second mate, — "Mr. Hanks, get the hook up."

The *Martin Connor* was as easy to handle as a perambulator. She would sometimes actually seem to wriggle her ugly little hull into places without orders once she understood what it was you wanted. I brought her over and under the coal tips as though she had been a canoe. She was a small iron tramp steamer, as unlovely as a factory and as sound as a bell. As well as being the means by which Captain Hawks (her sole owner) made his living, she was also his pride and his hobby, and he yearly spent upon her upkeep a sum of money that would have opened the eyes of some of these owners of six- and eight-thousand-ton tramps in the Western Ocean trade. And this was not because such a sum was imperatively necessary, but because it was Captain Hawks's positive joy to have an absolutely sound ship beneath him.

"Efficiency is my religion," he used to say, "and it's not a bad religion either."

The *Martin Connor* was an eighteen-hundred-ton tramp, two hundred and ten feet long, by twenty-nine feet ten inches in beam, by twelve feet three inches in draught, with an average speed of fourteen knots at sea. You will note from these figures that she was no *Aquitania!* But she possessed an equipment of labour-saving devices and working conveniences seldom found in ships five times her size. Amongst these must be ranked a most modern and complete set of engine-room auxiliaries, a searchlight (of a commercial pattern) upon her upper bridge, submarine signalling apparatus that alarmed us greatly until we got used to it, self-trimming hatches, electric light throughout, cold storage for ship's food, steam steering gear, of course, with screw gear aft, a direct steam windlass, a horizontal multi-tubular donkey boiler, some steam derricks for working cargo, a patent suction-working ash ejector that made a sound like a young earthquake and which was the pride of Mr. McLushley. But over the excellences of her engine-room I will not pause, as being too technical, though Mr. McLushley, whose every wish was gratified, would dissertate profoundly upon his latest acquisition, which was, if I remember, some single-action furnace fronts that "Gave a maxeemum o' pow'rr wi' a meenimum o' coal consumption, a larrge airr-cooled passage afforrd'n' a high furrnace eeffeeciency."

Somewhere in the business section of Galves=

ton Captain Hawks was tempestuously at work, and the results of his activity arrived in a continuous stream of articles to be prepared for and received by me. Nor were inanimate objects all. For shortly before midday there arrived on board a certain Captain Alexander Esterkay, an old friend of my commander's. He was coming with us, apparently, and he strolled aboard as though all eternity lay unruffled before him, followed by a very small boy who, in turn, was followed by two negro porters carrying dunnage. Captain Esterkay bowed to me with the utmost politeness (he was a Southerner of the most Southern), paid the negroes more than they were entitled to, and giving a bunch of keys to the very small boy (whom he called "Twocents") he bade him unpack the trunks.

The next arrival on board the *Martin Connor* after Captain Esterkay and Twocents, was a thirty-five-foot light-draught power boat, and with her came many barrels of liquid fuel. I had known nothing of this launch until she was on the wharf and a negro teamster was asking me where I wanted her, much as though he had brought a sewing machine or a typewriter. This evidence of hurry was no new thing with Captain Matthew Hawks, who, being shipowner as well as shipmaster, hated demurrage twice over.

"A motor boat?" I asked the negro, "for us?"

"Yes, sah," replied the teamster with the cheerful air of one who finds joy in presenting problems for other people to settle.

Had it been a giraffe stuffed and mounted, I would have accepted it and made preparations for its reception. So in due course the launch — a long, elegant, canvas-covered craft — was stowed away. Then came the liquid fuel and trouble in the shape of a hawk-eyed insurance official who quoted section A- this from section B- that with regard to the shipment of petroleum, paroid roofing, ferro-silicon, metallic sodium, and nitre cake. Apparently he was paid by the amount he talked, and I could have cheerfully heaved him over the side into the dock. But at length I stowed the fuel even to his satisfaction and we parted without unnecessary ceremony.

Few landsmen realize the amount of work which is entailed by the departure of a ship from harbour bound upon a long voyage. There is an endless procession of detail to be attended to — that must be attended to at once. The larger half devolves upon the mate, usually a much-harassed man who carries round with him a sheaf of papers in his hand, an indelible pencil behind one ear, and imperfectly concealed wrath in his bosom. My subordinate, Timothy Hanks, the second mate, was a concentrated product of

New England, a serious, conscientious young man without a grain of conscious humour in his composition. He was a splendid worker and never knew when he was tired — or, at least, he never let me know it, and I worked him hard enough! But final decisions must come from me, while there was the knowledge that I, in turn, was responsible to the captain. So I do not suppose that I was in a particularly good temper. What I might describe as a "ramping bustle" pervaded the ship, and, as a minor ill, there was a humming southerly breeze that swept all the litter and dust from the wharf on board and which smarted in the eyes and gritted between the teeth and was a continual source of petty aggravation.

All the same, when our new crew arrived, shepherded by their boatswain, — the latter the most gigantic man I have ever seen, — I had time to note, with a roving and preoccupied eye, how instantly, almost ferociously, they fell to work. Pausing a moment I wondered greatly where my commander had found such men. These were no sailors' boarding-house productions, mutinous and incapable, and with the single exception of the negro carpenter they were Anglo-Saxon to a man. Then I recollected the far-off and formidable Rio Maranon Rubber Company, and I smiled to myself. Such men as these were just precisely what a shipmaster would wish for when embarking upon an uncertain enterprise.

With such material to work with, a frenzy of industry possessed the second mate. Used to the necessity of driving his men, I remarked, with inward amusement, his puzzled and embarrassed air when all his orders were carried out with a clattering rush. He was even disconcerted as a man might be who, expecting to lift a weight finds no weight at all.

There was, of course, the small army of creditors to settle with, and I, owing to my long intimacy with my commander, was empowered to deal and dispute with them. Three dollars and seventy-five cents due for the privilege of warping a shore-line across somebody's frontage, somebody who saw in this the possibility of a gross financial gain; four dollars and eighty cents for a drum of particular paint; eight dollars for this; two dollars for that; ten dollars for the other; and one irascible individual who affirmed that the noise of our winches had frightened his horse which in consequence had run away and smashed up a new buggy, for which he was going to law to claim damages unless he got five dollars, cash down, on the spot in settlement. It did not take long to see him over the side, where he remained on the wharf shouting insults until our cook drove him away with lumps of coal delivered with remarkable accuracy of aim.

In the background of my absorbed perturbation was Captain Alexander Esterkay, a placid, bland, rotund figure, with a straw-coloured, sun-bleached, flowing mustache, soft Southern speech, and a never-failing politeness. He effaced himself with the great effacement of a ship-master in a vessel other than his own. He was a calm influence in that turmoil, an oasis of peace to turn to, a gently emphatic and positive proof that all was really well with the world in spite of misleading appearances. He gave me a most excellent cigar which soothed my spirits and which pleased the palate; which gave me a moment while puffing it to think before answering the never-ending inquiries. That is the practical assistance of a cigar!

Captain Esterkay was, in most respects, the laziest man on earth, and he was, also, one of the nicest. Throughout that cruise, even while piloting us in the Amazon, he sprawled away the hours in a deck-chair, a large, unbuttoned figure, blond and weather-stained. Somewhere hidden behind his misleading exterior there lurked an artistic appreciation for contrasts. This, perhaps, had more than a little to do with his un-premeditated adoption of Twocents, who was the very antithesis of himself. There had been generous motives at work as well, and an amiable vagueness of purpose. He had considered, no doubt, in an indefinite sort of way, that the boy would be useful to fetch cigars from the cabin, or his large green-lined umbrella which he used to protect himself from the disintegrating ferocity of a tropical sun, or just to sit about and listen while he talked, for that elderly and corpulent mariner was drawlingly garrulous to a degree. A malady of inertia had beset him in early middle life, when he had discovered it too much trouble to wear his false teeth, and the years spent in extra-tropical regions had but emphasized a strong natural tendency to sit in the shade between meals. Thus Twocents would be valuable to fetch and carry.

The boy was fifteen years old, and when he first came aboard he was incredibly thin and slight. His connection with Captain Esterkay had been effected through the medium of Captain Esterkay's peculiarly high-crowned straw hat which a lively trade wind had flicked from his pink bald head and set rolling down the street. Twocents happened to be near, and, hearing the captain's open offer of a nickel for his hat, had set off at once in chase, swooping upon the headgear as a hawk swoops upon a dove, returning with the captain's hat in the twinkling of an eye. This agility had so much

impressed Captain Esterkay, who found loco-
motion an irksome problem upon all occasions,
that the germ of an idea had come to him as he
changed the promised nickel to a ten-cent piece.

"Yo' kin move lively, s-o-n," he had remarked,
taking his hat from the boy and offering the
dime, while, with his kindly, watery blue eyes,
he had gazed downward over the horizon of his
rotundity and observed the fact that behind the
boy's street-bred alertness there had lurked a
nice expression.

"An' yo' look as though a meal'd do you no
harm," he had added. " Yo' a Galveston k-i-d?"

"No, sir, N'York," Twocents had replied,
looking very straightly up and grinning, while
the captain, with methodical force, had jammed
his high-crowned straw hat upon his head. "Yer
wants a string to that hat."

"I do," Captain Esterkay had agreed with
complete gravity; "but if yo' are a Noo York
kid, h-a-o-w —"

"Alston Beal's," had replied Twocents proudly,
but still grinning merrily, for it is possible for
some natures to grin with even an empty stomach beneath it. "The show broke up at Vicks-
burg," added the boy.

"O-h! Circus!" the captain had replied; "yo'
are a kid from a circus?"

"You got it," Twocents had answered, nodding his head briskly a number of times to drive the point home, and still smiling brightly.

"An' when the show broke up, did they just turn a kid like yo' loose to starve?"

"Yessir," Twocents replied cheerfully.

"Well, I gaise some folks jus' deserve all that's coming to 'em later on," was the captain's comment as the germ of the idea that had come to him grew towards hatching point.

"An' yo' folks all 'way, 'way off in Noo York?"

"Ain't got no folks," had replied Twocents, as though such were the happiest of circumstances.

"Are yo' lyin', k-i-d?" had enquired the captain with unmoved placidity, his blue eyes fixed upon the boy.

"Sure not."

"What was yo' in the show?"

"Number Two, Belsize Trio, Trapeze Artists," Twocents had answered with pride.

"Which means just acrobat, I s'pose. And ain't yo' got no place to go, s-o-n?" had then enquired the captain as the idea in his head hatched itself and came into being.

"Me and de gang sleeps around de wharves, mostly."

"I see, an' yo' will sleep in jail by 'nd by," was the captain's imperturbably calm reply as the idea in his mind now steadily approached the resolution stage. "Want something to eat, s-o-n?"

"Sure!"

"Then yo' come right along with me," was the captain's order as he got himself, in his high-crowned straw hat, his crushed linen suit, and his waistcoat of robin's-egg blue, in motion, and the boy, still looking upward and still grinning, trotted at his side.

Captain Esterkay marching, and Twocents trotting, thus made their way to an establishment where meals could be had for twenty-five cents, and full meals too. The place was called "The Mercantile," and it contained a free-spirited negro waiter, a reek of food, and a great buzzing multitude of flies. Twocents crowded in behind the captain, for owing to long intimacy with pitiless circumstances the boy entertained profound misgiving of ever receiving anything for nothing, and he therefore stuck close to his new-found friend and hoped for the best.

"Now, s-o-n —" had begun the captain, sedately revolving, while Twocents, anxious to follow wherever he might lead, revolved with him.

"Where th' mischief is . . . oh, here yo' are!" and the captain had laid a fat, sun-tanned, bleached-haired hand upon the boy's shoulder and had thereupon whistled loudly.

"Have yo' got no meat on yo' bones at all?"
he had exclaimed. Then, with sudden energy he
had thrust the boy down upon a wooden bench
facing a table stained with food.

"Sit and eat!" had commanded the captain,
then looked round with quick authority for the
free-spirited negro waiter.

To be confronted with evidences of privation
had made that placid mariner oddly angry, and
he hailed the waiter in a "maintop" voice. When
the negro arrived and was inclined to be imper-
tinent, the captain had promptly reduced him
to a simmering state of nervous obedience by a
full-toned blast of speech that must have proclaimed the captain's presence and profession
both within and without the building.

Twocents, in his own way, was an instinctive
judge of character, and after some years' lamen-
table experience in a third-rate circus his opinion of mankind could not be of the highest. But
in Captain Alexander Esterkay he had become
instinctively aware of a difference from the men
he was accustomed to, and this difference had
made the boy respectful, though hitherto Twocents had only been respectful through fear.

The captain, lighting a powerful cigar to save
himself a little from the reek of cooking, had
then seated himself with tender deliberation and
much caution upon an inadequate stool, and had

watched the boy eating while a new gravity came
to his kindly eyes. From the negro, who had by
then learned that it was best to hover at the
captain's elbow, he had ordered one dish after
another, and had thrust them across the table
to Twocents who had speechlessly absorbed the
food. Being by nature an easy-going man, this
spectacle of real necessity in a boy so young and
slight had caused the captain positive discomfort, and it had not been until Twocents paused
to breathe that the elderly man's attention had
relaxed. Then briskly demanding a fresh supply he had arranged the dishes in a tempting
semicircle and had coaxed in his soft, drawling
voice —

"Yo' eat some more, k-i-d. Don' yo' stop.
Keep right along now. This wedge o' pie?"

And Twocents, with his eyes fixed in solemn
resolution, had begun afresh, and the captain
had continued to watch with almost breathless
interest and anxiety.

But finally, the laws which ordain that the
finite capacity of any vessel is limited in proportion to its size, and that two or more objects
cannot occupy the same space at one and the
same time, had brought Twocents to a gasping
stop, and the captain, looking happy, had paid
the bill.

Outside in the clean wind and bright sunlight,

Captain Esterkay had breathed deeply. He was a man who appreciated more than a little the great culinary art, and he must have suffered considerably in that cheap eating-house. He had then looked down at Twocents, who, walking silently barefoot at his side, was experiencing for the first time in a considerable period the sensations of satiety. Something in the boy's obedience, in his taking for granted that where the captain led he must follow, and something too in his extreme slenderness, had affected the elderly man in a curiously emotional way. Captain Esterkay had never married; he was without kith or kin, and the possessive instinct within him had never been satisfied and was then aroused, almost assaulted, by the evidences of implicit trust in one whose whole appearance was youthfully pathetic.

"In five years' time he'll probably be no kind o' good to himself or any one else — that is likely," had thought the captain, "unless —" and the idea in his head had then arrived at the point of resolution with a rush.

Though I believe that Twocents spoke the exact truth when he said that he was without a home, the captain, with a large experience and a still larger tolerant understanding of humanity, had considered the statement open to doubt. But even if he had a home somewhere, the captain considered that its evidences were such as to justify the step which he was about to take, for with him, at any rate, the boy would be properly clothed and fed.

He would also be taught to work.

As clothing was the next item to be considered, the captain had then backed his tops'ls before an emporium where machine-made clothing festooned the front like banners in preparation for a civic procession. With unhurried precision he had purchased six small cotton shirts and three pairs of overalls, which last were of a comprehensive nature, having an upper extension and shoulder straps, the ingenious device, I believe, of a gentleman in Virginia. A warm jacket was added, and a pair of gum boots, some shoes and socks, and two canvas hats were added to the jacket, the whole being then made into a parcel and given to Twocents to carry in round-eyed silence, his usual street-bred glibness of tongue and quick impertinence suddenly deserting him before the captain's unruffled, uncondemning, and irresistible authority of manner.

"Now," had concluded Captain Esterkay, as he paused for the last time, "d' yo' want a job with me? Two dollars a week an' yo' keep?"

"Yessir!" had been Twocents's prompt reply, and less than an hour later they had come aboard the *Martin Connor*, followed by the negro porters carrying the captain's dunnage as I have described.

That is how Twocents came among us, and he stayed to win our affection and to lay for himself the foundations of a fine man and a sailor.

CHAPTER II

In the trying and intricate business of preparing the *Martin Connor* for sea, I had been greatly assisted by our cook, a cook for princes and a prince of cooks. He was a very old friend and attended to the stores himself. There was, therefore, a lot taken off my shoulders, for I knew that Wilfred Gee, or "Cert'nly Wilfred," as he was called, was more than capable of dealing with any victualling firm in Galveston or elsewhere. There are few firms, indeed, supplying the large orders given by ships for frozen meat, groceries by the ton, and other commissariat details, that can be implicitly trusted to give full measure in every particular of a list running into hundreds of dollars. A sack or two of flour, a pound or two of coffee, salt, sugar, or tea, is easily missed when these are ordered in the large quantities necessary to feed thirty-eight or forty men for a period of four or six months. In fact, though it may not be apparent, the victualling of even a small ship for a lengthy voyage, where no fresh supplies can be had with any certainty, approaches the region of science, and requires experience, accuracy, and thought. Beyond signing the necessary cheques, Captain Hawks never worried himself with this department, for my commander's method was to procure the services of the best men he could find, pay them well, feed them well, and shovel work and responsibility in full measure upon their shoulders.

It is a good system.

Before starting upon a cruise, Captain Hawks would summon Cert'nly Wilfred to the cabin, where the little man would arrive with notebook and pencil and a certain dry ceremony of manner; the proceedings then opened with the presentation of a cigar which Wilfred would adjust delicately behind his right ear to be smoked at a later date. With such necessary information as the probable duration of the forthcoming cruise, the probable risks of the cruise taking longer from unforeseen circumstances, and the possibility or otherwise of replenishing stores upon the way put down in his book, Cert'nly Wilfred would then retire to his own domain to work out his requirements. This done, the little man, in shore-going clothes and a hard felt hat, would sally forth to invite tenders and spend a merry day. He displayed the greatest acumen in setting one firm against another, in obtaining still further reductions in contracts, and in the minute and particular examination of every detail sent aboard. The stores were always right to the cent and the ounce, or, at least, the ship benefited by any error and never the contractor. And if any dispute arose, Wilfred would not come to me to settle it for him; he would settle it himself with the galley poker or anything else that was hard and handy.

Cert'nly Wilfred first saw the light of day in Hack Street, Tidal Basin, North Woolwich, London, E., and from an early date he was connected with the alimentary world. As first assistant to a cousin in the shrimp and winkle trade he developed a profound sagacity in the preparation and improvement of matter for human consumption, and at seventeen he owned and ran a coffee-stall just off the Shadwell High Street. It was here that he first saw the wide possibilities afforded by the culinary art, and in less than a year he sold his coffee-stall and pitch at a fifty per cent profit as being altogether unworthy of his talents. He could do better; he knew it, and he did.

As all persons of all ages and both sexes who reside and have their being in that district, of which Tidal Basin is but a particle, are connected either remotely or directly with the sea and ships, it was only natural that Cert'nly Wilfred's career should be flavoured by a strong marine influence from the first. A distant relative upon his mother's side (his mother was a large and generous-souled woman who never left London from the day of her marriage to the day of her death, fifty years of prolific and voluble life) owned and ran a collier brig from Newcastle, and in his humble coaster Wilfred, just eighteen, assumed his first position of sea cook. In a little under two years he dropped this, too, knowing this, as he had known the coffee-stall, to be unworthy of his talent.

Being by temperament one who makes either violent enemies or close friends, and being instinctively drawn to the sea, he next took charge of the galley in an ocean-going tramp, and made his acquaintance, at a larger salary, with the larger world. After a year and a half of this employ, during which time his natural gift for cookery had grown naturally and without effort, the ship fell in with the yacht of an American who owned more miles of railroad than he could hope to remember. The yacht had suffered during a prolonged gale, was in a sinking condition, and the immediate transhipment of her people was imperative. The transhipment was effected, and the family and friends of the millionaire suffered considerable discomfort in the rough surroundings of an English cargo boat. Not so the millionaire himself. It is a fact that men of resource and calibre, no matter what their nationality, religion, or manner of living, can always meet upon the common ground of their own strength of character, and the man of railroads found himself more thoroughly happy in that cargo tramp than he had been in his palatial yacht. The ship was real, her people were real, the millionaire was real — they understood one another. Being more than usually dyspeptic the railroad magnate, therefore, came in direct contact with the cook, who, being the artist he was, set himself to prepare nourishment which was not only digestible in quality, but was appetising as well. When the ship arrived at a South American port whither she had been bound, the man of railroads promptly offered Cert'nly Wilfred a prince's ransom in the shape of a yearly salary to continue preparing his food, which offer, of course, Wilfred as promptly accepted.

"Cert'nly," replied Cert'nly Wilfred with his usual familiar friendliness, and from thence onwards for three and a half years the little man saw a strange and wonderful life. Wherever the Prince of Railroads went, there also went the Prince of Cooks. But three and a half years of this employment was as much as Cert'nly Wilfred could stand. He must get to sea again, not in yachts and liners, but in the common merchant ships that wait not for fine weather, that are to be found in every quarter of the globe, that seek adventures upon deep waters, that acquire adventures in strange rivers, that have adventures thrust upon them. Those two, Cert'nly Wilfred and the railroad millionaire, bade each other almost a tearful farewell in private, and armed with credentials that would have gained him the position of *chef* in any hotel had he wanted it, and with a considerable sum in the bank, Cert'nly Wilfred wandered westward, seeing life. He chanced across a Texan with blue eyes, a large mustache, with a cattle ranch the size of a European kingdom and a forty-four calibre revolver hanging low down upon his right hip. Here again that subtle understanding that enables men of widely different birth and attainments to come together formed the basis of a friendship that was responsible for an invitation to see Western life on a cattle ranch in Texas, and Wilfred enjoyed himself immensely. It mattered not that he could not ride, it mattered not that he misplaced his "h's," it mattered not that he was small and undersized. For he had that which it is essential that all real men should have. As it happened that during his stay the Chinese cook inadvertently exposed his person in the track of a chance bullet, Cert'nly Wilfred readily filled the gap so caused, and though the materials which he had to work with were mostly of the canned variety, he executed miracles that endeared him for ever to those haphazard men of the West. It was here that he first became known as "Cert'nly" Wilfred, from his amiable habit of reply, and it is a remarkable fact that, though he was prevailed upon to stay over a year in the West, he never once bestrode a horse! He affirmed that he would be made seasick by the motion.

But in the end the sea must have him, and he was escorted to the nearest railroad by twenty-five men-at-arms who presented him with a brace of revolvers and a cartridge belt that were not bought for a hundred dollars. In San Francisco he chanced across Captain Matthew Hawks and settled down for life, a life that was as varied and unexpected as all things must be that are even remotely connected with that formidable Californian, a life, as Wilfred puts it, where "things 'appen." Wilfred here found the world wherein it suited him to dwell, and where it suited the world he should be. Vociferous and shrill, he guarded his employer's interests and lived a life that continually demanded of him his best. Despite his delicacy of health, he possessed a high and singular courage; irrepressible and bland, he was wholly without fear of life and without dread of death; with a keen intelligence, a generous soul, and with real artistry in his profession, he was an intrepid and remarkable little man. No community of persons could but be enriched by his presence, for he enjoyed a sound philosophy; no atmosphere so bleak but could be warmed by his disrespectful humour, and no situation so tense but could be partially relieved by his undaunted remarks. Such was Cert'nly Wilfred our cook, a great-hearted little man.

It was toward five o'clock in the morning before the *Martin Connor* was finally ready for sea. Captain Hawks arrived about midnight in one of his rather brutally cheerful moods, shouldering his way through those upon the wharf with a truculent disregard for those he bumped into. Clad in blue serge, his white-topped cap and white collar contrasting vividly with his leather-like complexion, he looked the large and vigorous man that he was, and one destined and equipped to force himself a place wherever he might be.

The clatter of our winches echoed loudly along the water-front as we swung out from the wharf; the perspiring stevedores scrambled ashore after eighteen hours' consecutive work despite the unions, while a lonely policeman stood yawning and watching our departure. It was a fine and merrily tempestuous summer morning, the Gulf wind already blowing steady and warm, a river of air streaming northwards to the hot plains of Texas and Arizona. The streets of Galveston appeared and disappeared like the spokes of a revolving wheel, and across the great arch of sky were hurrying clusters of brilliant clouds bowling swiftly inland, trailing after them their flying shadows that patched the sunny landscape. The fresh breeze rippled the tightly stretched awning above the bridge, and the even song of the happy engines running sweet and true under Mr. McLushley's fiercely loving eye came through the open skylights.

In company with a fleet of Gulf Fishery Company's vessels we swung down the Bolivar Channel. Beyond, the Gulf stretched dappled and glittering, windy, clear, and spacious, a sea of infamous memories. As time passed and we gained the open, the warm wind increased to half a gale, a roaring, tepid draught rushing inland to equalise pressures. Every stay, wire, and line upon the ship thrilled and vibrated, while the bridge awning rolled and rattled like a drum, and the brilliant sun deluged the flashing scene. Right into the eye of this fine breeze snored the *Martin Connor*, pitching and lifting rhythmically to the foam-patched seas, her heaving wake swinging out behind her beneath a fan-shaped spread of smoke, while a great concourse of birds followed for some distance out, twinkling and soaring in the bright sunlight.

A ship's course from port to port is a mathematical problem that bristles with technical terms such as "apogee" and "opogee," "loxodromic curves" and "diurnal parallaxes," "precession of equinoxes" and "equiangular spirals," all of which irresistibly suggest to my mind strange and highly eccentric animals! However, there are persons, mentally incomprehensible to me, who find the keenest joy in these regions, and my commander was one of those persons. Nearly all his spare time was absorbed in the compilation of technical works of reference for the mariner.

Hour Angles of Sun, Moon, and Stars; An Introductory Hand-book to Nautical Astronomy; The Adjustment of Compasses; A Manual for the Deviation of Compasses in Iron Ships, and *The Reduction of Lunar Observations*, represented the outlet which Captain Hawks found necessary for his restless intellect. It is, therefore, not to be wondered at that he took his departure from the beacons at the entrance to the Bolivar Channel, and laid his course and corrected it ("the course made good," as sailors call it after the adjustment of deviation and the variation of the compass and the computation of ocean currents and wind pressure upon the ship) with an accuracy that made it as mathematically correct as the longitude of Greenwich.

Had he kept this lust of figures to himself, I should have regarded his strange passion with detached and respectful interest, but, whenever the proofs of his books came in, and whenever he laid a course, my commander would ask me to "run" over his calculations and check them independently. As my "run" was at best a halting crawl, I would discover at intervals (while thus floundering in his wake) some detail concerning the ship which would call me away with a spinning brain to draw breath. In self-defence I must state that for all practical purposes my navigation is as sound as another's, and that I possess a "Master's Extra"; but I am content to leave my conclusions without carrying them out to ten points in decimals, and I can be assured of my own accuracy without proving my totals by half a dozen geometrical designs upon the chart like an overgrown cobweb.

In Mr. McLushley, our chief engineer, Captain Hawks found a kindred spirit, and though the regions of their investigations lay in separate departments of sea life, they yet met upon the common ground of accuracy — accuracy carried to an inhuman point. Mr. McLushley was approaching the age of sixty years, and until he entered the employ of Captain Hawks, he had never been long in one ship. He had passed a robust and stormy career making enemies and collecting all manner of certificates for super-competency. He was, on most occasions, outrageously rude, and shipowners who expected big dividends from unseaworthy ships, engined by machinery that should have long since been scrapped, were not likely to retain his services when Mr. McLushley did not hesitate to state, in rasping Scotch and with the greatest emphasis, the precise condition of their property, their base attitude of mind, their dishonourable methods of business, and what he sincerely hoped would be their personal future in this world and in the world to come. There are some things which it is not prudent to say, and Mr. McLushley said them, for he was one of the few men I have ever known who literally feared no one on earth excepting always a minister of the Free Kirk of Scotland. His usual manner was provocative of a breach of the peace, hence he was, in time, blacklisted by shipowners the wide world over, and he was found practically starving by Captain Hawks, one day, in San Francisco. Now, my commander is known and respected in that metropolis of the West; moreover, his size and general appearance gain him respect in most places. He was therefore not the least offended, but instead, very interested, when a tall, threadbare Scotchman, with whom he dropped into a casual conversation, contradicted him flatly six times in five minutes. Captain Hawks was not accustomed to being contradicted in just that manner and said so, whereupon the Scotchman had remarked that it was time he should be, whereat my commander had grinned friendlily and had said to himself, "Verily, this is a man."

Their remarks had concerned some machinery awaiting transhipment from the wharf; and even though the machinery in question was of a marine order, and though Captain Hawks certainly knew more about a ship's engines than most master mariners, he could not be expected to have an almost infinite knowledge and instinct of what was, after all, not the primal department of his profession. Furthermore, the mechanism under discussion was of a new and complicated nature, and as the casual stranger had demonstrated his points in long, carefully punctuated, broadly Scotch, and highly technical sentences, Captain Hawks had not taken long to realise that he had been wrong, that the stranger was right, and that the stranger knew a very great deal about his subject. Like most clever and enlightened men, Captain Hawks had at once admitted his error, and had then promptly asked the ill-clad Scotchman aboard to breakfast, commenting mentally, "I want this man and I am going to have him." The Scotchman had refused the invitation and had turned away with the air of one who has been asked for a loan. That was my commander's first meeting with Andrew Kinnaird McLushley, of Dunoon, Argyll, in the Kingdom of Scotland; and in the end, of course, Captain Hawks got his way.

There now existed an odd friendship between these two highly efficient, taciturn, and formidable men, a friendship that was not marked by any affectionate terms of speech or even uncommon civility. They seldom sought each other's society except upon the occasions when they would revel together solemnly in the regions of higher mathematics. For the most part they would actually seem to avoid each other, my commander never entering the engine-room of his own ship, and Mr. McLushley only mounting to the bridge when technical and official etiquette demanded, when his stay would be of the briefest, and when his manner would be particularly repellent. They never addressed each other by their Christian names, a certain unapproachable ceremoniousness always marking their intercourse together. Yet had they been separated by half the world, and had one of them needed assistance, the other would have come, at all cost, full speed to the rescue, when their meeting would have appeared anything but affectionate!

Nor was much geniality introduced into our

social atmosphere by Timothy Hanks, our second mate. Coming of a maritime ancestry from an austere New England stock, his dark hair and ripe-mulberry-coloured eyes an inheritance from his mother, a woman from the mountains of Auvergne, he was used to the very hardest conditions. Though he was one of those happiest of created things, — a man living for his work and not just working for his living, — his countenance bore an expression of foreboding doom, a besetting seriousness that is peculiar to youth in certain temperaments. Ever since he had first blinked his mulberry-coloured eyes at a New England winter day, life had been a stern reality. He had fought his way through the ills of infancy with a roaring voice; he had struggled through a few years of schooling and heroic disgrace for innumerable combats; and at the age of fourteen he had run away to sea in a New Bedford whaler where boys are cheaper than food. But in spite of disadvantages, or perhaps I might say with the aid of disadvantages, he had done well with himself, and now, at the age of twenty-two years, he was a second mate in steam and a first-rate sailor, albeit a solemn young man.

As I am approaching middle age, and am one not temperamentally hilarious, the sombre atmosphere was in need of relief, a relief generously

supplied with inexhaustible vigour by Cert'nly
Wilfred and Twocents. But no ship could remain a place of gloom with Captain Alexander
Esterkay on board. These three formed an adequate counterpoise to Captain Hawks, Mr.
McLushley, Timothy Hanks, and — well, yes,
perhaps myself!

From the first moment aboard, Twocents had
been consumed with curiosity concerning every
detail of the ship, as all right-minded boys would
and should be, and it had not been long before
he had discovered Cert'nly Wilfred tempestuously at work in the galley. That these two
should be friends was a foregone conclusion,
though for a time the little man's cockney dialect was somewhat incomprehensible to Twocents.

" 'Ere, Tiddlediwinks!" hailed Wilfred, and
fell at once to cross-examining with shrill questions. And Twocents, by no means emanci-
pated from his street life, had not unnaturally
answered back with some impertinence, only to
receive a sharp reprimand from the cook that
was physical in character, amiable in impulse,
and most successful in effect!

Twocents was startled.

In the wretched and sordid circumstances that
had encompassed him in the circus, he had often
both received and avoided a blow delivered with

ill-tempered ferocity, at which times, as could
only be expected, he had made liberal use of such
speech as he heard habitually used around him.
But never before had he received a clean, flat
smack, delivered open-handed, without malice,
and in such a location that only a considerable
stinging and no possible injury was the result.
The chastisement had been accompanied by a
cackle of laughter from the cook which had
robbed the proceeding of all suggestion of over-
emphasis, and for the first time in his short life
Twocents realised the possibility of justifiable
punishment, sane, tempered, and even affectionate.

It made a world of difference in Twocents!

I think we were all, in our different ways, un-
consciously grateful to that boy. In spite of the
cheerful influence of Cert'nly Wilfred and Captain Esterkay, there would have been lacking,
but for Twocents, that elusive element that only
youth can afford. A collection of adults, of
work-a-day adults, is all the better for that element, and whether Twocents was getting amiably spanked in the galley by Wilfred, or exploring the ship with a restless, pup-like energy and
a hair-raising nimbleness due to his acrobatic
training, he was generally in the back of our
minds. From the truck of our stumpy masts to
the stoke-hold Twocents possessed the ship like,

as Wilfred said, "a cat on 'ot bricks." He altogether defeated Mr. McLushley's forbidding grimness, and with the unerring instinct of a child beheld the man beneath, for though Mr. McLushley was feared by men, children and dogs gambolled about him.

But some forty-eight hours out from Galveston we began to forget Twocents, as a more serious matter arose out of the south and east to engage our attention.

There was, in the first place, what I might describe as a hesitancy in the usual trade wind, which finally ceased altogether some hours before it should have done, followed by an odd rise in temperature. As any departure from the usual in the weather, in the Gulf, especially at certain seasons of the year, is regarded by sailors with suspicion, this change was quickly noted by Captain Hawks, who, with his usual alertness, at once commenced a table of half-hourly observations. To add to our suspicions there began to come out of the south and east a perceptible cross-sea with no wind from that quarter to warrant its presence. This was toward midnight about fifty hours out from Galveston. I had risen to take my watch and had gone first, according to my custom, to the galley for some supper (or breakfast, whichever it might be called) which I knew would be ready and waiting. The night was placid and still, the black sky strewn with a multitude of stars, and in the windless space the smoke from the funnel hung about the ship, giving the night a reek of unswept chimneys. A certain stillness pervaded the atmosphere, what I might term an unhealthy stillness, and so warm was the night that I decided to stand my watch in my sleeping-suit without troubling to dress, only taking with me an oilskin coat for possible showers. Wilfred had not turned in; he never seemed to go to bed, and he was engaged upon the construction of a wooden cuckoo clock, for clock-making was one of his pastimes.

" 'Ere, Mister Mate," said he, with the affable familiarity that marked our intercourse when alone together, for we were very old friends, "where's this sea comin' from?"

"From the south and east," I replied stolidly, and blinking in the bright light cast from the electrics that made the iron galley as bright as day, and which was reflected from row upon row of copper pans graduated nicely according to size.

"An' what may be down theer?"

"Some kind of a breeze, I should judge."

"Feel 'er pitch ter thet, now?" said the little man, pausing in his work, his head meditatively upon one side, as though he were listening to the faint echo of some far-off sound. The ship took

three successive dives, not deep ones, but quick
ones that were peculiar in their motion, and not
unlike a smooth-running sledge that rocked
suddenly and sharply over three ice-embedded
logs. The movement suggested a very peculiar
wave formation.

"I knows thet lift, I do," said Wilfred, continuing with his clock-making; "I've felt it before,
oncet in the Formosa Channel"; and he turned
and grinned at me exposing a lonely tooth.

I was hard at work upon my bacon and ta-
males and the kind of tea one drinks when one
has a good digestion.

"I 'aven't bin goin' to and fro on this 'ere
world an' walkin' up and darn wiv my heyes
wide open wivout learning a thing or two, I
'aven't," resumed Wilfred, holding up to the light
a small piece of wood he was shaping. "Nor
'ave I bin at sea for a good many lively years
wivout becomin' acquainted wiv the motion of
ships, Mister George 'En-ery Grummet."

"We'll know all about it by and by," said I,
comfortably aware of a sound ship, a sound crew,
and a highly skilled commander.

"I think we will, even though there ain't no
'Ong Kong Water P'lice Station in the immeejit
neighbourhood to send up fireworks [1] by way of

---

[1] Three bombs and a black cross at the masthead is a signal
given by the Hong Kong Water Police Station indicating the
immediate approach of a typhoon.

"'ERE, MISTER MATE, WHERE'S THIS SEA COMIN' FROM?"

a gentle 'int to the mariner to shift 'isself over th' nearest 'orizon. The one I alluded to jest now, in the Formosa Channel, was full-powered enough fer me, I can tell yer. The velocity of the wind tetched a hundred and twenty odd, so I learned, arfter which it blew the wind-gedge away and went on increasing. Yer need a string to yer 'at in a breeze like thet."

The ship entered upon a series of short, high, sawing pitches, and for a time we said nothing, Wilfred at his bench and I at my meal both keenly aware of the movement.

"It's odd, y' know, jes' odd," remarked the little man thoughtfully without looking up; "it's an odd sea"; and I grunted in reply.

The galley, for cleanliness, would have done credit to a man-o'-war, though there was a homeliness foreign to warships that made the apartment characteristic of its occupant. Everything had a hook or a batten or a ledge or a wedge to hold it firm and prevent it from rattling or slipping in a seaway, and what free spaces there were were filled by photographic enlargements — for Wilfred was an excellent photographer — in frames bolted and screwed to the bulkhead. To one side a door opened to the little man's living quarters with "OFFICE" neatly painted upon it, the light through the doorway revealing a shelf full of account books above a locked desk. Here was to be found an exact record, in a sloping and laborious handwriting, of every ounce of food purchased for and consumed within the ship. At one side of the desk was Wilfred's bunk, with a set of drawers beneath it. The photographs in this apartment were of a more personal nature, being mostly family portraits, and several views of Hack Street, Tidal Basin, North Woolwich, London, E. Thus, above his bunk was a painfully enlarged portrait of Wilfred's mother, smiling down, large and amiable from the stern of a waggonette with a background of Epping Forest. And about both the galley and his living quarters there was a great ticking of clocks that chimed, struck, and cuckooed uproariously together at every hour and half-hour.

I finished my meal and nodded to Wilfred.

"Good-bye, darling," said he; "what a wonderful thing it must be ter stand on the bridge at midnight an' control the workin's o' —" But by that time I passed out of hearing.

I found Timothy Hanks marching up and down, vigilant, solitary, perspiring, and gloomy. He paused at the ladder-head and looked about him as though now that his watch was over he discovered himself to be a human being.

"It's very warm, sir," he remarked in even tones.

"It is, Mr. Hanks," I agreed. "You might even call it hot," said I, lighting my pipe, and for a moment or two we both watched the flame of the match that fluttered only slightly with the movement of the ship. "And there's no wind," I added, flicking the match over the side.

"No, no wind," he repeated thoughtfully. Then after a pause he added more briskly as he turned to go: "Good-night, Mr. Grummet; I think I'll sleep in my clothes."

Throughout my watch the conditions steadily worsened. Before daybreak I noted that the stars no longer shone with their usual clear metallic brilliance, but with a distorted sheen, like lights beheld through a smeared window pane, with long points emanating from their centres. The heat was extraordinary and most oppressive; the sea grew higher and changed its course slightly toward the east. The sunrise came late, masked by a heavy bank of cloud that lay like solid land upon the southern horizon. Even when the sun rose clear of this, its direct rays were veiled, as by a film that painted the dome of sky a pale blue. And the quality of the heat was that of an enclosed space, as though the world were roofed by a semi-transparent substance which, while permitting the sun to pierce it, prevented all wind from penetrating.

The calm was more than a calm; there seemed to be actual absence of air, and the entire atmosphere impressed one as hanging poised, awaiting some cataclysmic happening.

CHAPTER III

A TEST FOR SHIP AND SEAMANSHIP

TECHNICALLY, a typhoon, hurricane, or cyclone is known as a "revolving," or "circular," storm, and the handbooks in their cold, unimaginative fashion dissertate in measured tones upon their construction and cause much as medical works will discuss some ravaging sickness.

These storms have, in addition to a motion round a centre of low barometer, blowing more or less a circular course, a progressive movement along a straight or curving track. They revolve against the watch hands in the northern hemisphere, but with the watch hands in the southern; and the indications of their approach are the threatening appearance of the weather, a heavy swell not due to the wind then blowing, and above all to a falling barometer, "or even if the regularity of its diurnal variation be interrupted, danger may be apprehended."

There you have a technical description of the conditions in which a West Indian hurricane may be expected, and it is strikingly inept. One is led to picture the mariner, manual in hand, regarding his coming extinction with a detached spirit and an observant eye, coldly in search of self-improving knowledge.

It was not in this admirable spirit that Captain Hawks and myself regarded our conditions, the conditions surrounding the *Martin Connor* at that moment entering the Straits of Yucatan. We had closely examined a small scale chart of the Gulf of Mexico and the table of figures compiled with care and accuracy by my commander throughout the preceding hours. The ship was stripped of her awnings, and everything moveable was lashed and counterlashed, fixed, stayed, and bound in every way that ingenuity and experience could suggest. The heat was tremendous, and out of the south and east came those great walls of water, unbroken, and growing steadily larger as time went on, moving silently immense, and sweeping the steamer up and down with a swinging motion so great and so steep that it was next thing to the impossible for a man to move without hanging on to something. Yet there was no breath of wind. The sea had the appearance of cod-liver oil; it seemed almost sticky; and its weight and impetus, and its smooth, vast, oily-silk undulations were unlike anything I have seen. It was no longer like water; one could imagine it the liquid substance of some other world, strangely convulsed by some wholly unearthly commotion.

The surface was unbroken and showed neither ripple nor foam, and the waves came moving swiftly sedate in a silence that was most disconcerting; it was, as Captain Hawks said, a wicked sea.

Our study of the chart was interrupted by a whistle from Timothy Hanks down the bridge-tube. I answered it.

"A British man-o'-war a few points off the port bow, sir," said he, "and she is flying some signals. But as there's no wind I can't make them out."

I repeated this to the captain.

"Step out with the glasses," said he, "and as soon as you can read me out what she's saying"; and he reached for the bookshelf above the desk, his legs spread wide to steady himself.

I hooked my elbow round a funnel stay and raised my glasses. Out of the curious haze that hemmed our horizon to the limits of a few miles, I beheld a great grey war-vessel flying the White Ensign. She was heaving prodigiously, the centre of a vast acreage of white foam; for she was cutting athwart the seas which climbed all over her, giving her the appearance of a half-tide rock. The flags she had mounted hung limp and undecipherable, only shaking out a little as the ship rolled. I called Captain Hawks to come and look at her, for she was a fine sight.

"Big lump of a ship, that," said he; "I wonder what she can want with me."

Just then, the Britisher, to attract our attention, shrieked mournfully on his siren. As we approached closer to each other I made out the patches of bunting.

"Two red flags, sir," said I, — "two red flags with blue or black — no, black centres and a red pennant. She has two black cones up, the cones are base to base."

While the captain was turning the pages of the signal book I shifted the glasses to the warship's upper bridge. She, like us, was stripped of her awnings, and all over her main-decks the sea was streaming in white cascades amid the complicated litter of polished accoutrements. Her strange deck-fittings would appear and disappear like rocks upon a beach in a heavy surf, and even her big guns would sometimes dip out of sight, for they had been lowered as much as possible to diminish the roll.

"Two red flags with black centres," said Captain Hawks, "displayed one above the other, indicates the immediate approach of a hurricane. The red pennant displayed with the flags gives the direction; red means easterly to south. That is American. The cones are British," — and I heard him slap another book down and run over the pages. "Two black cones mounted base to

base means the immediate approach of a typhoon. He'll have got that by wireless from
Havana, Grummet, and he's making dead sure
that I'll understand and so puts it up in American and British. Onto the bridge with you and
Morse him, 'I understand,' on the whistle. Then
run up the Stars and Stripes and dip them, for
I am much obliged for his politeness."

The moment I whistled (a long and a short, a
long and a short, a long and a short, a long and
a short) the flags came down smartly, man-o'-
war fashion, but the cones remained up. When
the Stars and Stripes dipped, he Morsed, "Give
the girls my love," and so we parted.

"Well," remarked my commander, "he's con-
firmed my suspicions. That little show of bunting of his, translated literally, means: 'If you
ain't a criminal lunatic you'll get hence and out
of this,' which is just precisely what I'll do. He's
got the reliable information that this thing is
coming out of the south and east, and it'll be a
full-dress cyclone when it arrives. It is travelling at any rate you like in a northeasterly direction; and it will, at a point we can't determine,
incline east'ard again, according to its habits and
customs. Our new course is therefore westerly,
south of Yucatan, for ten or fifteen hours' steaming. That'll put this sea abeam and we'll roll like
our British friend. Better let McLushley know."

I followed Captain Hawks onto the bridge and I blew down the engine-room tube, then placed my ear to the mouthpiece. There came the heavy, irregular song of the engines, strangely concentrated in the narrow confines of the tube. Then the whistle at the other end was removed, the sound grew louder, and then was thrust aside, as it were, by the voice of Andrew Kinnaird McLushley.

"Well?" asked the Scotchman irritably.

"The course is to be changed," said I; "this sea will then be abeam. She'll roll, Mr. McLushley, she'll mighty near roll the funnel out of her. The captain wanted you to know."

"Did the captain think I'd be seasick?" was the answer, and the whistle was jammed back with such violence that it was like a slap in the ear.

All the same, I heard his warning cry, hoarse as a crow, to his second, who was doubtless lying prone or hanging acrobatically, oil can in hand, amid a maze of flying machinery.

Captain Hawks had stepped to the binnacle and was only waiting until I had finished speaking to the chief.

"All right, sir," I said, and the captain's eyes turned to the swaying compass card, while the man at the small steering wheel, with his bare feet planted far apart upon the grating, had the expression of one who is about to be tried for his life. For it is nervous work to be within a few feet of so august a personage as your captain, who narrowly examines your work, that, in itself, depends upon a circular plate of mica with a ruby in the middle and a tendency to swing right round with the violent motion of the ship. Your "average" may not agree with the captain's and there is no talking back or explaining at sea. The *Martin Connor's* compass card was graduated in degrees at the edge to obviate any reference to points and to simplify the application of deviation. In giving the new course, Captain Hawks gave it in points, and the man, repeating the order as the rule demands, pushed the wheel over. The ship took a dive like a man casting himself down upon his shoulder, while a half-humorous, half-surprised yell came from the galley where Cert'nly Wilfred made frantic efforts to save a pile of plates. The ship rose streaming with water from her fore-deck and heeled over prodigiously, and another yell and another tinkling crash of crockery came from the galley followed by the voice of Wilfred raised in disrespectful enquiry as to what we on the bridge were trying to do with the ship. But the following moment all sounds were obliterated by a second wave that came over our bows in great solid masses of water. For some seconds I lost all sight of the ship forward except for the fore-mast, while the tepid water swept ankle-deep over the bridge itself. The sea drained off and the ship rose again, and Captain Hawks himself steadied the wheel with one mahogany paw upon the spokes.

To change your course in such a sea requires skill and some nerve. The man at the wheel had his mouth shut like a trap and his bulging eyes fixed upon the card. With controlled frenzy he instantly obeyed the captain's second command, a command voiced in a quiet tone as though he were navigating a river, and once more the little ship went down by the head under countless tons of water. But this time there appeared to be two waves, one practically on top of another, or rather just behind, and therefore hidden.

"Look out, sir!" I yelled, and grabbed the sturdy, pillar-like stem of the engine-room tele-graph.

That sea swept the ship, — it was a monster, — and I do not know just what damage I expected. But as the ship cleared herself, there came the reassuring and distant vibration of the engines as before. And that sea had done us a service, for we were now right round upon our new course. Captain Hawks, wet to the middle, took half a dozen running steps like a slack-wire artist and whistled down the engine-room tube,

A YELL CAME FROM THE GALLEY

bringing himself up with an arm about a stanchion. As he did so we commenced a series of rolling wallows that cast the bridge from thirty degrees one way to thirty degrees the other. It was tremendous rolling, and we were going to roll worse.

"How much is she doing, Mr. McLushley?" enquired my commander politely, then clapped his ear to the tube.

"I want all that you can give me," was his next remark; and the water, for the moment being free from the decks, and with the entire absence of wind, his voice had the odd effect of echoing, as though from a low, roof-like sky.

"Do just as much as you dare," he continued; "I'm going to run for it if I can. Yes. Very good. What? As you say. Perhaps. Yes, came a mucker changing course. Yes, bad sea."

Almost at once a feather of steam appeared at the escape in answer, representing Mr. McLushley's power in reserve, though had that white plume appeared under ordinary circumstances there would have been words of a personal nature in the engine-room.

Timothy Hanks arrived, though it was his watch below. He appeared round-eyed but calm. He took up a position at the end of the bridge with his lips tight shut, and a memory of days gone by returning to me I drifted down to Timothy, beginning, as circumstances permitted, a desultory conversation upon technical matters; and his face relaxed a little, under the influence of human intercourse. I was a young second mate myself once, and I had not forgotten my own sensations when I was, for the first time, in a ship in great peril.

Wilfred, dripping wet and cheerful, arrived to report (according to custom) much havoc in the galley, and a vast quantity of crockery smashed to little bits. As there were others present, the little man made his report to the captain with precise, official solemnity, but his antics in keeping his balance were delicately exaggerated, and as he departed he made way for Captain Esterkay with a deference that was just a fraction extravagant. The rotund and elderly Southerner, for once agile and swift in his movements, inclined his head slightly in reply to Wilfred's bow, and a most unofficial wink passed between those two widely different men. For Captain Esterkay knew by instinct with whom he could be familiar. Having locked away a very seasick Twocents he came to give us the moral support of his presence — a master mariner well used to these regions and not altogether unacquainted with hurricanes.

The sweat stood upon our faces from the heat and the exertion of endeavouring to remain upright. Wandering flaws of oven-hot wind came eerily out of the gathering dusk with a sighing moan that startled the nerves already painfully stretched. The sea began to lose its wave formation, and in the early afternoon it was heaving up and down in pyramidal masses that shook one's faith in the ship, for the ship was hustled about like a child in a crowd. The scene was most sinister. It was like a picture of the end of the world. It was alarming by all tokens and strangely unnatural.

We were doing our best to get out of the track of the approaching avalanche of wind, but we could not have been very far from it, as was evident from the condition of the sea. Following a curving course, this storm of madly gyrating wind set up a tremendous sea, first in one direction and then in another, as it pursued its way. These different seas conflicted with one another, which is, I presume, the explanation of the conditions we were then in, for I have never seen the sea behave in that startling manner before (or since), though Piddington speaks of a similar sea having occurred once to his knowledge in the Indian Ocean. The heaviest North Atlantic gale, or the severest conditions that I can recall while running the easting down, are nothing compared to that sea just south and east of Yucatan which we experienced. For in a gale, no matter how strong, there is sanity and reason in the ferocity of the sea, a ferocity which a full-powered, well-found steamer is equipped to meet. But that hurricane sea was essentially extraordinary in so much that there was no wind to blow it *down*. It was prodigious and startling, and none of the recognised formulas held good. The water toppled aboard us from all sides and sometimes from all directions at once. There was no meeting it, no avoiding it; it thundered down haphazard as a building collapses, all ways at once, as though intent upon sinking the ship by sheer weight.

We on the bridge could do nothing; our fate was in the hands of Mr. McLushley and the good men with him. All the engineers were on watch together and there was a double crew in the stoke-hold. At rare intervals Captain Hawks communicated with Mr. McLushley and the chief's answers were short and to the point. He gave his reports in an irritable manner, technical and very Scotch, as though the strain of the moment had carried him back to his boyhood, and he were once again in a ragged kilt and with bare legs in that robust land of cold rain and rushing, porter-coloured mountain torrents.

The engines were behaving "sweetly" and true was ever the gist of his communications. He could keep this up indefinitely: —

"Though Gude kens this is no ordinair sea, an' the coal consumption is awfu'!"

"Never mind the coal, Mr. McLushley, please," replied Captain Hawks, always courteous and almost blandly calm. "You have got it there to burn, and I guess my General Average policy should cover the undue consumption anyway. It's a shocking sea."

"An' the glass, captain?" came up the tube.

"Both of 'em as low as I have ever seen and going lower, Mr. McLushley."

"Cree-ation!"

"Unless I can get out of the way we are in for something big."

"Wharr d'ye calculate is the centre o' this thing?"

"Forty miles or so sou'east, travelling nor'-west. I figure on it being well abaft the beam now."

"That'll put these seas astairn, by 'nd by, eh?"

"It should, but they are coming every which way now."

"Ye can feel them strikin' her doon here as though she warr landin' her forrefoot on a rock. She'll draw something. These are no ordinair condeetions. Are ye getting smashed up much?"

"No, nothing considerable. No more than a few hundred dollars worth of deck-fittings. But I can't see much of my ship."

"Very likely! Any one gone overboard?"

"No. Any one hurt with you?"

"Na, not yet, but they are fearin' a coal-slide. They are a wee bit jumpy, ye ken, no' mutee-nous, but just uneasy; ma second had to do some hitting foreby they answered back, but they are right enough at bottom. It's the heat, an' the heat in the stoke-hold is prodeegious, it's bad enough in the engine-room. One man's sprained his wrist, but he's shovelling awa' all the same."

"What man?"

"Yon rough tyke from the East Side, Carter."

"I'll remember."

I caught occasional glimpses of our gigantic boatswain. He resembled some powerful, slow-moving, heavily agile and semi-amphibious creature as he clambered about the ship labori-ously upon the alert. He was several times com-pletely submerged, but he was always there when the sea drained off, and in the calm perti-nacity of purpose he impressed one as being the embodiment of some invincible force that would win, and which was bound to win — in the end, no matter what happened now.

He was a fair-complexioned man, almost an albino, and at all times he moved with a meas-ured, unhurried competency. He was dressed in much-washed overalls that now, soaking wet, clung tightly to his splendid limbs. He was a gigantic man, and his muscles moved like oiled machinery, precisely, accurately, inevitably; without apparent effort, springing into being or sinking into quiescence beneath a tanned skin of polished rosewood. He wore a small, neatly trimmed mustache which he sometimes fingered with a massive hand. His eyes were china-blue, and his expression was that of a nice though rather stupid child. He was an Englishman, and in time every one in the *Martin Connor* copied his method of speech when addressing him. This had come about humorously at first, but soon became an established custom. It was characteristic of the two men that we should amiably poke fun at the boatswain's speech, though he was the largest man in the ship, and never so much as dream of doing so with Cert'nly Wilfred who was the smallest. The boatswain was known as " 'Arry Ketchold," for, in giving orders or instructions all that was necessary was to point and say, " 'Arry, ketch 'old," and whatever it was that 'Arry caught hold of was bound to come away or break. He was as handy to have about as a portable steam winch or a dockyard crane, and though he moved slowly he worked with a sustained and untiring industry, and with the same irresistible appearance as an elephant. He spoke in a soft, sing-song voice that was pleasant to the ear, and like many large and powerful animal organisms he was of a mild and gentle disposition. That he never took offence at the mimicking of his accent or at the practical jokes that were played upon him was due to his innate sweetness of disposition and as well to his size and extraordinary muscular development, for he had little need to care for his own dignity. A blow from his fist would have been like the kick of a horse; he knew it and every man in the forecastle knew it, and therefore 'Arry Ketchold had never need for a blow, and blows, I fancy, were not unknown in our forecastle, our crew being what they were.

The watch were clustered about wherever they could find a comparatively safe perch, and, as is the habit with physically fit men well used to a dangerous life, they were as uproariously merry as a picnic party, and were betting their wages on just how long the ship would float after the hurricane had overtaken us. There was not a distraught nerve among them, and well paid, well fed, and well worked, sound in wind, limb, and digestion, they would have been equally unabashed on Judgment Day.

Captain Hawks, grave and alert, with slightly corrugated brow stood clutching the bridge rail thoughtfully watching his ship. At intervals he

swung himself ape-like down to the charthouse
to consult the barometers, and a slight shake of
his head to me when he returned would mean
that low as they were they were still dropping.
We were playing tag with a cyclone, and the
game was becoming long-drawn-out. The course
was changed slightly to the southerly, yet the
conditions remained the same so far as the sea
and the absence of wind were concerned. No one
thought of meals, of course, though Wilfred,
with his heavy weather doors shut, had prepared coffee and a hot stew for any one who
chose.

The little man paid frequent visits to the
bridge-deck below us, and he took his life in
his hands every time he did so. He remained
wet and cheerful and vastly interested, as indeed this was an uncommon experience for any
man. The ship behaved as well as she could be
expected to behave. The conditions were such
that one felt that no ship could continue to live
long, no matter how well built, nor how skil-
fully handled. And then, toward five o'clock in
the afternoon we approached our nearest to the
cyclone. The wind came away suddenly. We
heard it coming before it arrived, and the sound
of its cataclysmic approach was awe-inspiring.
It was a combination of a deep, booming note
in which was discernible a high, penetrating

whistle and a great hissing. Its onslaught was the swiftest I have ever known. One moment it was a dead calm, and the next the air had come upon us like a landslide, and the bare steamer heeled over like a sailing vessel struck by a ferocious squall. Yet this was only the outside shell of the real hurricane, a mere flick of wind, as it were. It was at this moment that the barometers touched their lowest.

With the coming of the wind we five men upon the bridge lost touch with one another. The night descended soon after with a blackness of black velvet and added to our isolation. Savage daggers of lightning raked the southern sky, illuminating a really terrific scene. The sea was now one mass of white and roaring like Niagara. Our helplessness upon the bridge was now complete. We might have butted end on into a continent, a reef, or another ship. The spray was not spray, but solid sheets of water that drove across us and high over the ship in a manner no man could face. Crouched and clinging, we could not even communicate with the engine-room. At times the bridge was swept, and the weather cloths, long since gone to ribbons, gave no shelter from the sustained onslaught of the wind. There was nothing left for us to do but continue to persist, to persevere, and to trust to the good men in the engine-room, to good materials and good construction. I hung on in a not altogether unpleasant state of semi-coma. It was an unnatural weariness, but not precisely distressing; I found no great objection to drowning, at that time, for our circumstances were so overwhelming that drowning appeared a relief. No landsman can realise the effect of over-exposure in such conditions; it leaves one, in time, after many hours, without any particular desire to live or dread of death.

Dully I wondered how the others were getting on. Mr. McLushley and his engineers would be hard at it as they had been hard at it for the last twelve hours. In the stoke-hold they would be shovelling as they had been shovelling coal for the last twelve hours, and occasionally Mr. Mc-Lushley would make his dangerous way from the engine-room to the stoke-hold and demand more steam, and he would probably have a spanner in his hand to emphasise his demands, for the men would be dog-weary and perhaps a little mutinous and dazed.

I wondered idly where the watch had got to, and I wondered what Cert'nly Wilfred was doing. As a matter of fact, as I learned later, the little cook was seated in his "Office" smoking, and, wedged tightly, was listening to the insane tumult without and wishing that there was something to do.

At some indefinite time later, I became aware that Captain Hawks had left the bridge. He announced his return by yelling in my ear: "We have done it! The glass is rising!!"

We had dodged the hurricane.

CHAPTER IV

A DIFFERENT WORLD

IT is only to be expected that a mathematical maniac such as Captain Hawks should exercise the greatest nicety in making his landfalls. He prided himself upon being able to say, toward the end of a voyage, "At two-fifteen to-morrow morning we will raise the Leghorn Light and bring the island of Gorgona abeam"; or, "By three bells this afternoon Trincomali will be two points on the starb'd bow"; and I have seldom known him wrong. There are a few occasions, however, such as any sailor, no matter how skilled, can call to mind with a shudder down his spine, when an odd combination of circumstances, such as currents not marked upon the chart nor mentioned in sailing directions, and a faulty taffrail log, together with a persistent fog, has, sometimes, a really astonishing result, a result undreamed of by the underwriters of ships. These incidents a shipmaster keeps to himself, but he cannot keep them from his mate! Thus, one time, on a voyage from Bahia to New York, Captain Hawks and myself were completely lost (as it afterwards turned out) for over

twelve hours! It is just as well that landsmen
should realise that the captain who loses his
ship is not necessarily incompetent, and to recollect Lincoln's remark that a man who could
not make mistakes could not make anything!
At the end of long and carefully compiled calculations, worked out independently of one another, we pricked the ship off within range of
Cape Henry Light. Then the fog lifted and we
found ourselves *inside* the Diamond Shoal Light-
vessel off Hatteras. We said nothing on account
of the man at the wheel, but, like the parrot in
the story, we thought a good deal!

The town of Para is sixty miles from the mouth
of the Tocantins, by which the Amazon is entered, and the Tocantins Estuary is, roughly,
two thousand miles and some odd hundreds
from Galveston, U.S.A. The trip should have
taken from seven to nine days, one way or another, but the hurricane upset our calculations,
and it was not until the dawn of the seventeenth
day that a smudge upon the horizon denoted a
tree-smothered island and proclaimed us to be
a good forty miles up the river. With the sight-
ing of that island, Captain Alexander Esterkay
heaved himself from a deck-chair and took
charge of the *Martin Connor*.

On the forecastle-head, beneath an awning, the
watch below and the watch on deck sat about

more or less unclothed. From time to time a man would pull off what few garments he happened to be wearing, and a friend would lower a bucket over the side, and, after examining the water minutely, would pour it over him, then the man would try and find a draught to sit in. We had double awnings over the bridge with a foot space between them, and large canvas ventilators, swaying slightly from side to side and oddly resembling immense, dead, white sharks, communicated what air there was to the stokehold.

The island drew nearer and was a dull-green solid substance at rest upon a mud-coloured ocean, and another island took its place ahead. Except for those two spots and the colour of the water, which last had been fresh and more or less poisonous for the last twelve hours, the ship might have been in the middle of the South Atlantic. Twocents, in his comprehensive overalls and a shirt, raced about with bare feet and got smacked by Captain Esterkay for not wearing a hat in that murderous sun.

"Don't yo' go round without a hat, s-o-n. D' yo' want to die right off?" he enquired with some emphasis.

Captain Hawks, in a thin linen suit, reclined in the deck-chair vacated by Captain Esterkay. Timothy Hanks was below trying to sleep, and

I strolled leisurely up and down the bridge
glancing automatically ahead. On the after
main-deck Cert'nly Wilfred had fitted himself
up a carpenter's bench for clock-making purposes, outside the galley and beneath his own
particularly private strip of much-patched awning.

Our deck-fittings, though guaranteed for
North Atlantic winter weather, showed unmistakeable signs of what the ship had been through,
though the engineers, under the direction of
Mr. McLushley, and with the assistance of Andrew Jackson Jefferson Davis, our negro carpenter, and 'Arry Ketchold, the boatswain, had
worked miracles. If you turn loose a highly
skilled and qualified engineer, with materials, a
forge, steam power laid on in pipes like water,
with clever assistants and a gang of muscular men
well used to handling weights at the word of
command, you will see iron and steel worked
and moulded like so much putty; you can, in
fact, stand back and behold wonders. The job
had appealed to Mr. McLushley; he had fallen
upon it with a cold, glittering lust in his red-
rimmed, fighting eyes while Captain Hawks and
myself had, so to speak, taken a back seat. Bent
and twisted iron had become straight, fractured
steel had been collared and bolted at cunning
angles and served with wire, and wherever a

"D' YO' WANT TO DIE RIGHT OFF?"

wound had been, a skin of healing red paint covered the repair. During this process the ship had rolled over tropic seas vibrating loudly to the music of beaten metal. But there was a legacy left us by the tornado that Mr. McLushley could neither remedy nor even discover. The *Martin Connor* was taking in a good deal of water.

Now, all ships leak more or less, and the *Martin Connor* was no exception. The leakages, ordinarily small, found their way to the bilge, which was pumped out every so often by the pumps connected with the engines. But this was no infinitesimal inflow and was a matter for consideration. The violent handling which the ship had undergone had strained her somewhere. At first we had thought little of the water, as we had imagined that she had taken it in from her decks, and Mr. McLushley had promptly pumped her dry, only to find, next day, that there was again an unhealthy amount of water swilling round between her skins. Where, precisely, the leakage was situated, it was impossible to say, though the chief, in a shocking bad temper, spent most of a day "man-holing" with an electric torch. He had emerged dripping with sweat and bilge, scratched, bruised, and bleeding, and he made his report to the captain in a manner which my commander would not have allowed from any one else on earth. But the business of examining a ship's bottom from within, while at sea and in tropical regions, is almost a desperate undertaking. It means hours spent in the dark, in a suffocating temperature, with the possibility of getting drowned like a rat in a drain. It means frequent and complete immersion in evil-smelling waters, and all the time it requires skilled and vigilant observation. Mr. McLushley would send no one but himself, though he had three highly qualified assistants, and that success did not crown his efforts did not make him any more pleasant to deal with. The social atmosphere of the engine-room was, so to speak, tense. The lithe and muscular assistants went about their work with silent alacrity and with only partially concealed nervousness. When he had carried his explorations as far as it was humanly possible to do, Mr. McLushley appeared from the black depths that had swallowed him for so many hours, where warm, oily waters rushed with hollow, booming echoes, and sat himself down, grizzled and dripping, on the edge of a yawning hole and wiped his face with a lump of cotton waste handed him in sympathetic silence by the first assistant. Official etiquette would have allowed Captain Hawks to remain upon the bridge, the coolest place in the ship with the exception of Wilfred's refrigerator, but no one knew better than my commander just when and how to unbend from the exalted position of shipmaster. The subtle compliment and courtesy paid him by the captain's personal visit to the engine-room was not lost upon Mr. McLushley, but the chief was too Scotch to be over-polite in return.

"Ye'r a fine man an' a sailor, Captain Matthew Hawks," said he, gazing upward grimly, "an' it's ye'r meesforrtune to ha' been born a Yankee instead o' Scotch."

Captain Hawks waited with shut lips and with a smile somewhere in the background of his expression.

"We are takin' in watter to the disgraceful tune o' some ten to fifteen gallons perr hour, an' the leakage will, in a' probabeelity, increase to an enorrmous extent. Wharr it is I canna' say; how caused I dinna' ken; an' to put it precisely, I know no more than I did this morn, an' neither do you."

Captain Hawks nodded. "Have a cigar?" said he.

"Ah!" replied the chief, and with a begrimed thumb and second finger (the first had long since been missing at the joint) he picked a cigar delicately from the captain's extended case. The first assistant offered a match with zealous attention, and for a moment Mr. McLushley smoked in silence while the grimness of his expression relaxed slightly under the soothing influence of really good tobacco. Then, rising, he began to divest himself of his shirt and trousers, his sole articles of clothing at the time.

"I have," said he, his head on one side to keep the smoke out of his bloodshot eyes, "some pumps that will throw a sizeable stream. There is no eemmeediate cause f'r alarrms."

He was, by now, standing a picture of thin, hard, rust-streaked bone and muscle turning black and blue from bruises. He was, as Captain Hawks said afterwards, no drawing-room ornament, but he was all of a man.

"I'll go an' have a bath," said he, "an', MacPhail, you tell yon oiler to cast this dunnage o' mine overside. When I am clean, Captain Hawks, I will make ma full report in pairson. But at present I stink like a polecat that has been living doon a sewer, an' I am no fit company for myself, let alone ither folk."

So much for the leak, and it remained to be seen if it would develop into anything serious. It was just one of the many difficulties that assailed us upon that cruise, a cruise that will always remain in my mind as one beset by the unexpected. For, looking back, I now realise how greatly we had underrated the vindictive power and malignant attention of the Rio Maranon Rubber Company, and that so essentially sound a ship as the *Martin Connor* should be damaged by a hurricane *en route* seemed a gratuitous blow of ill-fortune.

As the day progressed, a haze upon the southeasterly horizon told of the river bank. Now, in regarding the Amazon, — or Amazonia, as all that vast country that is alternately flooded and drained by the Amazon River is called, — it is necessary to clear the mind of all previous ideas concerning rivers. The navigation of the Amazon is unlike all other river navigation on account of the scale in which Nature has chanced to plan things, and as well the proceeding is accompanied by incidents that are bizarre, to say the least. Thus, you will have an ocean-going steamer porting her helm to avoid a floating island populous with monkeys, or a four-thousand-ton tramp from New York, Liverpool, or Antwerp a thousand miles inland from the sea, with alligators rubbing against her anchor chains.

No one in the *Martin Connor*, with the exception of Captain Alexander Esterkay, had ever been up the Amazon before, and for us there was a continual entertainment, and an endless procession of daily incidents that were interesting, if not always of a pleasant nature. Captain Esterkay knew "the stream" as far as Achual

Point, — twenty-seven hundred and eighty-six miles from the sea. And he had been higher, penetrating, in fact, right into the remote inter-Andean plateau toward Lake Titicaca in Southern Peru. How so lethargic a man had accomplished such really prodigious journeys, accompanied, as they must have been, by all manner of bodily risks and extreme discomforts, I was, at first, at a loss to understand. And then, even before we arrived at Para, I understood. Captain Esterkay, whom I had considered the laziest man on earth, had a strange and passionate interest for and understanding of Amazonia and all it contained, much as a man can have a passionate interest in, say, oceanography or extinct civilizations. And certainly he knew a very great deal about the country in an instinctive way. He could tell you things that are not written or writeable in books; he told us things that would not be believed by the people who have never been more than a hundred miles from a street lamp, a barber shop, or a policeman. But we believed what he said. We just sort of knew he was right.

By daylight upon the following morning we raised Para, or, to give it its full name, Santa Maria de Nazareth de Belem do Grao Para, and shortly after sun-up we dropped anchor and awakened the echoes with our whistle. A launch flying the Brazilian flag came fussing out to us, and the customs authorities boarded us with the lust of piracy in their eyes, while Wilfred, who knew a thing or two, went round locking doors. From the ship Para appeared quite a town, with street-cars and public buildings. A closer look with the glasses showed up an avenue of mangoes and a lot of narrow streets beyond. It appeared a flat spread of dilapidated houses with here and there a palm tree in their midst. Gaily painted boats came out plying for hire, but we had the launch swung out and down which caused what Wilfred called "'ard feelin's" and some remarks until a few well-aimed lumps of coal from the jeering cook taught them better manners and that discretion is sometimes the better part of commercial enterprise.

We were to be joined here by the official director of the Rio Maloca Rubber Company, to the up-river headquarters of which we were consigned. I remained in charge of the ship, so I cannot describe Para from personal inspection, though Timothy Hanks, who went ashore to send picture postcards to a girl in New England, had little to say concerning the place except that it was very unlike Boston! But from those who went ashore unpleasant news began to sift through the ship concerning fever, and there were some really preposterous stories: stories of cargo boats rotting at their anchors up-stream with a forecastle full of the dead and dying. To these stories we paid as little attention as we could, though some of them had an unpleasant substantiality which was inclined to affect the crew until a large English steamer, one of a regular Liverpool line, came slam-banging past us, bound a thousand miles up-river, with a "time-is-money" appearance, and due back in Liverpool upon a schedule as fixed as that of the New York Central and Hudson River Railroad.

Captain Hawks was away early on business; Captain Esterkay, accompanied by a restless and excited Twocents, went later; and in the afternoon Cert'nly Wilfred went ashore to buy a hat. The launch was here manifesting its usefulness and playing ferryboat over the two-mile stretch of coffee-coloured water to the shore under command of 'Arry Ketchold and a deckhand. Wilfred returned toward evening, not only with a new hat, but with a shocking black eye and a large — medium-sized dog of no known breed. The dog had rough, short, wiry red hair, an exceptionally intelligent face, a very serviceable mouthful of teeth, a torn ear, and a tail that was neither short nor long. Wilfred had christened him "Stadger" and had acquired him from his former owner by violence. From what I could gather, and from what I could surmise, a considerable dust-up must have occurred, and in this wise.

Wilfred, promenading affably in a new hat of vast dimensions, heard the high-drawn scream of a dog in pain. Now that is a sound which no decent man can hear without protest. Wilfred protested. He protested with his right thumb under the left ear of the former owner of Stadger, who was vigorously engaged in beating the dog to death for having stolen some meat, a costly luxury in Para. Portuguese as spoken in Para was incomprehensible to Wilfred, who knew only emphatic cockney English, but he gathered from the group of men surrounding the dog that the punishment of being tied to a post and beaten to death was mild enough as judged by the natives of Para, since dogs have no souls and since their bodies are cheap. Cert'nly Wilfred is a very small man; he is small and delicate; but rage filled him as he projected himself like a missile and smote the dog-owner as I have intimated with much force and scientific accuracy. It is a paralysing blow, that of the thumb under the ear, when correctly administered, and the assault being unexpected, confusion ensued; confusion that attracted the wandering attention of an American seaman who was ashore from an American tramp at anchor in the roads. At that the dog showed its unusual intelligence, and perhaps he had a long bill against his master. At any rate, Stadger seems to have realised that rescue was at hand and that his rescuer was that most subtle being, a dog-person, or person understanding of and understood by dogs, for Stadger did not hesitate to throw in his forces with Wilfred, as soon as Wilfred had cut the cords that lashed the dog to the post. The former owner of the dog had folded up on the ground, but his friends surrounded Wilfred with drawn knives in a threatening ring. At this juncture the American sailor arrived, a large and effective man quite disposed for a row on general principles. Wilfred, with his back to a wall, and with the dog at his side snarling at their enemies, was hopelessly outclassed, but the little cook was guying the crowd in the highly personal fashion of East London. The American was not slow in realising the situation and that another white man was in for real trouble, though apparently wholly unabashed. He came to the assistance of his blood-brother in a silent and business-like manner, and began hitting in a ding-dong, unhurried way with a full-sized pair of fists at the end of a full-sized pair of arms. At that the situation became more or less acute. Wilfred, the American, and Stadger were, as the little cook put it, "all in." But they got out, and Wilfred, the American, and Stadger thoroughly enjoyed themselves in doing so. The end came with the arrival of some municipal guard, or police, and the three had to run to avoid getting locked up. They arrived in the central part of the town, where, having outdistanced the pursuit, they sat down, drew breath, shook hands, quenched their thirst, and licked their wounds respectively. That is how Cert'nly Wilfred acquired Stadger, and how it was that Stadger became a responsible and much appreciated member of the ship's company.

Captain Hawks returned after dark, and with him came the director of the Rio Maloca Rubber Company, who was coming up-stream with us, and my commander did not seem quite at his ease. The director, who rejoiced in the name of Alonzo Makepeace Massingbird, struck a false note in our company; I was aware of this from the first, and it explained the constraint in the captain's manner. Mr. Alonzo Makepeace Massingbird was a small man, suspiciously dark in complexion and fundamentally flashy. He belonged to an altogether different world. He reeked of cities and doubtful commercial undertakings, and he wore on and about his person some jewellery of no mean order. There was about him an assumed suavity, and his mobile mouth was scored about by betraying lines that suggested a "ready-to-wear" and shark-like smile. In the midst of this sham and pretence his tired eyes looked forth infinitely weary, wholly disillusioned, and perpetually suspicious.

Speaking metaphorically, Mr. Massingbird deluged us in rubber and financial matters generally. He ate rubber, drank rubber, and breathed rubber. He was one of those maniacs with but one idea, possessed by but one object in life, which all his thoughts, aspirations, and actions obeyed. And his object in life concerned rubber and rubber shares. Never have I met a man more destitute and blind and deaf. All that has gone to make this world and universe, and all that this world and universe are going to make were as nothing to Mr. Massingbird. Even the rubber itself was nothing to him; it was only the money he could get from rubber and the manipulation of rubber companies that engaged his life and what may have stood for his soul. Nor did he mind how he got the rubber, that was the trouble, and with the advent of Mr. Massingbird I became gradually aware of trouble somewhere vaguely ahead. Had I known how terribly he was to affect my own life, I would have left the ship at Para. To get rubber, or rather to make other people get rubber for him, and to sell it at a huge profit for a steaming six months of the year, then spend his outrageous profits in Paris, was Mr. Massingbird's reason for existence, and he could not understand us, who, in a very short time, could see no definite reason for Mr. Massingbird's existence at all. At first I listened to him with some awe. Such terms as "first mortgage debentures," and "cumulative preference shares," "bank bills," and "brokers' deposit rate," and such like incomprehensible things fell as easily and glibly from his lips as a man might speak of upper-topgallant braces, as though they were everyday matters, which, I suppose, they were to Mr. Massingbird. He could not, in the least, understand Captain Hawks's attitude to us, nor our attitude to the captain. To Mr. Massingbird any one in command must necessarily be hated. The smart discipline of the ship, the independent, uncivil, and prompt obedience of Mr. McLushley, the genial familiarity of Cert'nly Wilfred, the subtle give-and-take between Captain Hawks and Captain Esterkay, were utterly incomprehensible to the director of the Rio Maloca Rubber Company. The noble idea that is behind real sea discipline, that robs servitude of all servility and which dignifies command, was as the fourth dimension to that mixture of South American-ated Goth, Semite, and Vandal known as Alonzo Makepeace Massingbird. He may, of course, have been a very acute business man, but I don't like business men.

So the first meal on board the *Martin Connor* in which Mr. Massingbird participated was rather a stiff and formal affair. He endeavoured to dominate until he caught Captain Esterkay yawning behind his sunburned hand which disclosure caused that amiable Southerner (who was the soul of politeness) much embarrassment. But Mr. Massingbird was no fool, in many ways, and perhaps I should not criticise him considering what happened, but he made us all uncomfortable, for, after the discovery of Captain Esterkay's yawn, — and it was such a wholehearted yawn, too, — Mr. Massingbird realised that he was not appreciated and so dropped into a sudden and suspicious silence, with his head, no doubt, full of all manner of absurd reasons for our lack of interest in financial affairs!

The meals in the cabin were usually happy and jovial. Wilfred, as I have said elsewhere, was a cook for princes. There was always a steady flow of conversation and generally an argument, and the arguments extended over a wide field and might concern the heeling error of compasses or the best method of growing pomegranates.

There was some complication over the matter of pilotage which was handled by my commander in his usual rather sweeping manner which did not endear him to authorities. Certain Brazilian regulations demanded Brazilian pilots, but Captain Hawks would have nothing to do with either, snapping his fingers at both, and rather unwisely wagging the Stars and Stripes in the face of the river authorities. But at that time we none of us had any real notion of the full power of the Rio Maranon Rubber Company, nor how minutely they were watching us. Voluble torrents of language flowed from the authorities, and Captain Hawks chose, with great deliberation, a fresh cigar. The authorities danced and waved their arms, and the captain lit his cigar. The authorities pirouetted in extreme agitation, and the captain laid his heavy hand upon the bridge telegraph and swung it clattering down to "Stand By." The authorities left, fulminating, when we were under weigh, and the disturbance of our passage through the water and their own clumsiness nearly capsized them, to our grinning entertainment. A freshly peeled onion, aimed by Wilfred, called down upon him an official rebuke from the smiling captain, but the onion caught a Brazilian in the eye, all the same, and must have hurt, too, judging by the smack of impact and his loud, explosive yell. Thus we left Para, in no very good case to ask for protection from the Rio Maranon Rubber people, had we wanted it.

The Amazon River is not entered by its natural mouth, but by the Tocantins Estuary. This is because of a vast expanse of sand that has heaped itself in the mouth of the Amazon and over which there sweeps a bore wherever the soundings are not more than about four fathoms. This wave, at the precise instant when the inflowing tide overcomes the river current, advances at the rate of from ten to fifteen miles an hour, and varies in height, reaching as much as twelve and fourteen feet in places. As the Amazon is about one hundred miles wide at its mouth, this wave must be worth seeing and hearing, and is quite in keeping with the general scale and character of things in that part of the world.

It was therefore not until some time after leaving Para that we were genuinely in the Amazon proper, though Amazon conditions soon made themselves apparent. The first of these was the sudden descent upon the ship of myriads of insects that hummed, buzzed, piped, droned, stung, crawled, walked, hopped, and flew in uncounted multitudes, in your bunk, clothes, books, food, and, worst of all, about your person. First one, then another of us would start and clap his hand to himself with a crack like the report of a pistol and with a little remark that needs no repetition; or would start rooting beneath his clothing with one or both hands while an expression of growing alarm would spread across his face. The first creature to arrive was a monster with many legs, a spiked helmet like a German soldier's, a fully equipped stinging outfit which he manipulated with great skill, and the greatest conceivable energy. This thing arrived droning like a biplane and — according to Wilfred — barking like a dog.

There were others!

Wilfred ceased making clocks in his spare time and started collecting these creatures, and the larger and more deadly the captive the greater and shriller was his joy. From the captain he obtained some insect-killer, and with this on cotton waste in a pickle jar he made a killing-bottle. Thus armed with this engine of death and accompanied by Stadger, he busily stalked big game about the ship at all hours of the night and day. By some miracle of dexterity he was not only highly successful in his hunting, but, for the most part, he escaped unstung. In forty-eight hours he collected a nightmare series of the most shocking-looking insects I have ever seen. Later on, when we were really up-country and where wild animals abounded, the little man endeavoured to collect what he was pleased to call a "mangery," by which I think he meant menagerie; but he was reluctantly forced to desist in obedience to a strongly worded pro-

test, delivered personally, from every man in
the ship from the captain downwards. By some
odd chance his usual ill-health, his bronchitis
and asthma, from which he suffered continually in temperate and healthy climates, seemed
to improve in the most intemperate and unhealthy climate of the Amazon. It is sometimes
the way with small and delicate men, and so it
was with Wilfred, though his well-known cough,
which sounded so like a man beginning to sing
into a jug, remained as much a part of the ship's
sounds as, for instance, the song of the engines
or the rattle of iron shovels from down the stoke-
hold ventilators.

The Amazon is connected with the Tocantins
by a maze of incredibly deep, natural canals,
and it was a new experience to go swinging down
these narrow water lanes at full speed with the
trees almost brushing our sides. And the trees
were immense. They were not, of course, like
the giant redwoods of California or the giant
gums of Australia, but the uniform height of the
forest was twice that of any forest I have seen
elsewhere. As I have said before, the *Martin
Connor* was as easy to handle as a canoe, and, in
fact, Captain Esterkay twisted the ship about
very much as though she had been one. There
was no break in the forest wall except where
other waterways branched off, and over some of

the more narrow of these the trees stretched in leafy tunnels. The verdure rose straight from the water, the water as often as not disappearing into the forest, the waves cast up by our progress breaking and swirling in and around the huge tree-trunks. Thus one got no sight of the earth itself; the earth was covered and smothered beneath tepid water and chaotic vegetation. Occasionally a snowy heron or cygnus would be disturbed by our approach and would rise and fly on ahead and settle down, only to rise again as we drew near. It would take a far better man than I am with a pen to describe the first impression of the Amazon. We all exhausted our vocabulary of exclamations in a very short time. We had imagined a larger river, or, rather, we had imagined the largest river we had ever seen magnified two or three times. We were therefore surprised and perhaps disappointed when we emerged finally into the Amazon proper to discover it no bigger than the Mississippi. The reason for this was that we did not see it all, its full width being masked by countless thousands of islands.

There were canoes and river schooners and wood-burning steamers, most unseaworthy-looking craft and most clumsily handled and laden to the water's edge. The languid, half-clothed men on board them did not seem to mind what we said to them through a megaphone when they did their best to be run down, but then, perhaps, they did not understand. It was here that we first encountered the real Amazon smell, a smell that was to remain in our nostrils long enough to plant itself in our memories for the rest of our lives. It was a smell that was not unpleasant; it was subtly attractive, strangely reminiscent, and exceedingly sinister. At a remote period of time our ancestors must have known that smell well enough, that thick odour of primeval rot! Doubtless our forebears sniffed it and found it good. Or more likely they never noticed it as they swung gaily from tree to tree. It is therefore a matter for nice conjecture how and why it was that the Amazon smell seemed vaguely reminiscent and familiar! Its subtle attraction may also have been due to an unconscious awakening in us of a long-forgotten sensation of the nose! Its unpleasantness at times was due to our delicate and super-refined modern nostrils, and as for its sinister quality, perhaps, again, it awakened within us the rapid flights of fear, the knowledge of perpetual danger, the low cunning and alert suspicions of the little monkey men and women of the coal age! But these may be fantastic imaginings. I yet maintain, however, that the Amazon smell does, indeed, affect a man of any perception in an odd way, which, I am convinced, strange as it may sound, has more than a little to do with the shocking change that creeps over a man, almost any man, after a prolonged residence in Amazonia; which is, to a certain extent, responsible for the iniquitous individual engaged in collecting rubber there. This statement may sound preposterous, but if any one laughs too loudly at these remarks, be he a minister of the Gospel, a scientific man with reasons for everything, or just an ordinary kind of a man, let him go and live for a few years in the upper Amazon region. Unless he is a man in ten thousand, such a period of residence will work in him a truly diabolic change.

CHAPTER V

IT was I who enjoyed the undignified and unpleasant distinction of being the first to go down with fever, and Amazon fever is a particularly violent and pernicious edition of ordinary malaria. Standing in the charthouse writing up the log, I had occasion to look at the clock and I was surprised to find that I could not read it. I stared at the well-known, bald, white face and thought confusedly. I could not remember which way the hands went round. My head ached severely, and I felt as though I had swallowed a steam radiator and a lump of ice; the two seemed to be fighting for supremacy. I stood and stared at the clock and was aware of a gradual darkening about me, as though the sun had been obscured by the passage of thick smoke. I glanced out of the thick, plate-glass charthouse windows and observed that the river tilted uphill at a surprising angle.

"Something wrong," I commented; "rivers should n't do that sort of thing. Better tell the captain." And forgetting all about the half-written log, I mounted to the bridge one step at a time and there stood swaying and clutching the rail.

Captain Hawks was, I think, deep in a game of chess with Captain Esterkay. He was always playing chess with Captain Esterkay and always getting beaten, which fact gives, to a nicety, the two temperaments of the men in question. My commander glanced up and stared emphatically while some one who had borrowed my voice shouted from a long way off that the river was running up-hill. The captain rose hurriedly and appeared swaying before me.

"You go and turn in, old man," he said; "go at once, and I'll mix you one of my special quinine mixtures."

The sky turned black and the trees turned white and I found myself being embraced by the captain. There then followed vast journeyings in space. I visited the outer stars, I rose to prodigious heights, and like Tomlinson, I dropped sun by sun to abysmal depths. My steering gear gave me constant trouble; I found it frantically difficult to answer my helm, and only by the very hardest work did I manage to miss hitting some terribly large stars. I worked till the sweat rolled off me in rivers while I yet shivered in absolute zero. When I awoke wearied out, I was aware of great distress — a vague and terrible mental distress and a sound of wild tears and horrible anguish. But the distress vanished before the old and reassuring familiarity of my cabin and the sight of Cert'nly Wilfred. No angel could have appeared sweeter than he, to me, at that moment. He was bathing my face.

" 'Ello!" said the little man briskly; "Grummet's come back! Wheer yer bin, George?"

"Just there and back," I answered weakly, "but it's a long way. Give me something to drink."

He handed me a glass of tepid water which I swallowed at a gulp.

"Like soapsuds goin' darn a drain," commented the cook.

"Some more," said I, "and put some ice in it."

"No hice fer you, me boy. Hice is ag'in' orders. What abart a drop of tea, old dear?"

Gradually I got better, but I was five days doing it, and I returned to duty to find the ship well up-stream.

There was no alteration in the scene. It was the same immense river that in places widened to great lagoons. We were still steaming along the left bank, the right or northerly bank being often but a thin blue line upon the horizon, and there was the same maze of islands fringing the shore.

To a man who endeavours to describe the

conditions prevailing in the Amazon Basin, there arise almost insurmountable difficulties of language. A man might possibly experience the same trouble did he try to describe a personal visit to the moon. Unless the reader is ready and prepared to accept certain fantastic facts for granted and is fully aware that the region under discussion is a preposterous enormity of Nature, mere words are inadequate. The Amazon is out of scale with this world; it belongs to a much bigger place than this pill of a world of ours. At some incomputable period of time, ages and ages and ages ago, it is thought that the Amazon Valley was an inland sea rather smaller than the Mediterranean, or, to bring it home, about as large as from Chicago to New Orleans one way and from New York to Omaha the other. Into the western end of this sea flowed a river that rose amid the Andes, and the Andes were probably much higher then. They have been whittled away, so to speak, by rain and melting snow. Through countless ages that river, laden with a rich deposit, formed an ever-widening delta. This delta in time — there was no hurry in the process — levelled up the depression in which lay this great inland sea, and while doing so the river cut a passage for itself through its own deposit. Thus, so it is thought, was the Amazon Basin formed. Now, however, the Amazon is not a river, it is a vast body of water extending for thousands of miles over an almost level floor of ooze. This area, three quarters the size of the United States, extends and contracts according to the seasons. At times it overflows and spills out into the unexplored forests for unknown distances, and covering this region, alternately flooded and partially drained, there extends a matted tangle of vegetation that defies description. Hundreds of thousands of channels, ditches, and waterways cut and wind in every direction, and in this debatable area, half land and half water, darkened to a deep and steamy gloom, there dwells, in a state of perpetual warfare, a swarming multitude of animal, insectile, and reptilian life. And all this is bathed, soaked, and permeated by a dripping malarial climate that waters the very heart out of a man and which rips to pieces his moral and nervous system. Seldom is there an inch of earth revealed to the eye, and to move from one place to another a man must go in a boat. One seldom ventures into the forest; Nature forbids it; and a few yards from the river it remains as unknown to the white man as it was in the days of the Pyramids.

Timothy Hanks, an industrious young man ever in search of information, had been at some pains to discover the different names and natures of the plants that composed that ocean of vegetable growth. I fear that I am more indolent, or perhaps I care more for the forms of things than for the names given them by man, though it is true that I got to know a tree fern from a silk-cotton tree, and I learned what a Brazil-nut tree looked like, but the latter was owing to happy memories of *Charley's Aunt.*

The sense of sinking deeper and ever deeper into this strange, mysterious, and wholly sinister country was oddly insistent, and affected a man with a feeling of growing remoteness which the very infrequent settlements did nothing to dispel. The traffic on the river was growing less day by day, yet the forest and the river remained ever the same, as unaltered and gigantic as the sea.

The captain was pursuing a diligent enquiry for some news of his partner, Colonel Ezra Calvin. At Para he had heard nothing, though an interview with the American Consul there had added to my commander's fears for his partner. The up-river country, according to the Consul, was entirely in the hands, official and unofficial, of the Rio Maranon Rubber Company, and any man, no matter of what nationality, was as good as dead if he made an enemy of the all-powerful Rubber Trust. In such a country there are many ways of killing a man, either by an arranged "accident," or by deliberate shooting; while, at the best of times, any man might disappear through perfectly natural causes. Just in what way the colonel had got on the wrong side of the Rio Maranon people was a mystery, though I gathered from what I had heard of the colonel that diplomacy was not his strong point; while the sight and knowledge of injustices provoked him to the openest of open speech. And we were beginning to realise that "injustice" was too mild a word for certain conditions existing in the rubber districts far up-stream. As yet, however, these were only rumours, unpleasant to hear or contemplate. But the fact remained that the very worst spot in the whole wide world for a cantankerous, strong-willed American to visit was probably the Upper Amazon country, especially if his avowed intention was to open up a trade route in competition with the Rio Maranon Rubber Company.

One of the most essential accomplishments for a sailor to acquire is that of sleeping at any time and of being able to wake at any moment. As the navigation of the Amazon by seagoing ships is possible only in daylight, all hands, with the exception of a watchman, turned in at night on board the *Martin Connor*. Yet I do not think that the majority of us slept very well. I would lie in the thick hot darkness, counting the passage of the night by the regularly recurring bells struck by the watchman on the bridge-deck, and by the simultaneous uproar from Wilfred's collection of clocks in the galley; these last were surely strange sounds to be echoing through those Amazon nights. Between-whiles I would listen to the multifarious and sustained hum of countless insects, the shrill treble of the mosquito being accompanied by a great variety of unknown basses. These flying pests had outrageously venomous notes, formidable and vindictive, and there was always the lively possibility that one or more would, with diabolic ingenuity, wriggle and squeeze himself through the mosquito curtains that surrounded the bunk. At intervals the darkness palpitated ominously from sheet lightning that flickered in the black depths of the sky.

Then there was the unnatural stillness to disturb one. There was no sound of wind, no harbour sounds, no sound or motion of the sea; it was fantastically as though the ship were afloat in empty space. Then, to shatter a rather pleasant fancy, would come an entirely unknown sound from the forest close at hand. Now, a sound is often not disturbing when it is familiar, or when the cause is known; but when both sound and cause of sound are wholly unknown and strange, and often of a most tragic suggestion, then your eyes flick open to wide-awakeness and sleep kicks up her heels and runs away.

Those night sounds from the forest were strangely disturbing. They were peculiar and intense; they suggested the turmoil of war, of life preying upon life in a never-ending series of horrible and fatal surprises in the unwholesome darkness of that rank, rotting world of strangling vegetation. They sounded oddly wicked; they played upon the nerves; they got hold of that remnant of the frightened child that there is in every man and basely attacked his reasoning faculties; and that Captain Esterkay, who had travelled far in this country, could not explain the cause of half of them, added greatly to their power to disturb. I read far into those Amazon nights, and all that I read has remained in my mind mixed with the stagnant strangeness of that wicked river.

Wilfred also was a poor sleeper; moreover, as I have said before, he never seemed to go to bed. As every door was hooked back for better ventilation, a light from within shone out as a beacon offering the possibility of companionship to the sleepless. Thus, after a time, I would hear a soft tread in the alleyway, and the little cook, bland, thin, and amiable, clad in pyjamas and smoking a cigarette of strong, rank tobacco, would stand smiling at the door, and, owing to the intervening folds of mosquito curtain, robed in a certain stage-like mystery like the ghost of Hamlet's father!

Gradually the iniquitous night would pass, and toward morning there would rise a thick malarial mist. Its coming would be unnoticed until, glancing up from the pages of my book, I would see the grey masses drifting down the alleyway past the door. At five o'clock the man on watch would ring the bell violently, perhaps in joy that his duties were over, — and really I did not envy that lonely man, — and yawns and mutterings would come from open doors, together with the cheerful crackle of burning wood from the galley. A little later and the odour of coffee and frying bacon would drift through the ship, and with the lights turned on we would sit down to breakfast in the cabin.

Breakfast over, it would be light enough to get under weigh, and Captain Esterkay, followed by my commander, would mount the bridge-ladder while I went forward onto the forecastle-head. The mist at that time was usually rising from the river as steam rises from boiling water, the growing daylight half-revealing the banked mass of foliage that marked the wall of forest.

"Break her out," would come the captain's quiet voice, non-personal in its official intonation.

Instantly the roar of the steam capstan would shatter the morning stillness to little bits. Leaning over the rail I would watch the cable come up dripping link by link, while a man with a long pole would disengage from it the festoons of derelict growth, and while strange, excited fishes would swim round in consternation at the phenomenon. Those fishes held a strange fascination for me. They suggested, as indeed was so, a world of blood-warm water teeming with voracious life, rank, poisonous and dangerous. I would not, for worlds, have fallen into that river! As the anchor appeared, — heavy, covered with grey sticky mud, untroubled by the stinging death around it, a foreign thing forged in the cold, inevitable North, — I would sign with my hand, and the uproarious capstan would cease its triumphant song of power, and while the forest flung back the echo I would call, "All clear for'ard, sir!" and the engine-room bell would ring out loudly, hurriedly commanding, from the open engine-room skylights. The reply to the bridge would come; a shudder would pass through the ship that became, in a moment, the accustomed vibration, and the iron bows, festooned with the anchor awash, would part the sluggish stream. Thus the day's work began.

Our progress was a zigzag. Captain Esterkay would take the ship from one side of the river to the other, often without apparent reason, while Captain Hawks would stand or sit at his side an interested spectator. There could be no complete or definite knowledge of such a river. The navigation of the Mississippi is conducted in much the same fashion, though, of course, upon a smaller scale.

As gradually the great Amazon engulfed us, it became more and more apparent that wherever the romance of our destinies had taken us before, we were now in a world of extravagant incident. Perhaps the most conservative thing extant is a ship, clinging as she does to the early Norsemen in her very nomenclature; but apart from this, she is intended to meet and compromise with the heavy violence of the seas, while every detail of her construction speaks eloquently of her readiness for combat with the unstable waters. Therefore there was something humorous in the *Martin Connor*, with her stout iron and steel fittings, with her compact solidity, with her staid and robust utilitarian character, disturbing somnolent alligators with her wash, or anchored amid a field of water-lilies and surrounded day after day by an impenetrable forest festooned with priceless orchids, populous with monkeys, and the home of the wildest life. It was like going to Central Africa in a street-car.

The fact that we clung to the ship as though she had been in mid-Atlantic was also part of the extravagance. We continued steaming as long as it was light; there was therefore no chance to go ashore by day, and not even Wilfred suggested a trip ashore by night. Therefore we made no closer acquaintance with the low-lying "igapo," or flood lands, for some time. Here, in the gloom of the forest, lurked various forms of unpleasant death. In these flood lands, often inundated to a depth of fifteen feet in the rainy season, and for the most part bottomless morasses in the dry season, was a swarming world of reptiles, and some of the snakes were credited with appalling length and power.

Quite unexpectedly, as far as appearances are concerned, we came upon a mud-brick, bamboo town standing between the river bank that was here raised a few feet, and a low line of bluffs about fifty feet high a little way back from the river. Behind the bluffs was a line of low, rolling hills, the first land we had seen that was more than a few feet above the uniform dead level of that gigantic valley. The river also narrowed here to a mere creek a mile wide, but was, in consequence, of tremendous depth. We passed on, greeting this ramshackle town of Obidos with a friendly blast of the whistle. The forest took up the sound and flung it contemptuously back at us as we steamed on into the great wilderness. Surely a strange experience this, for an ocean-going ship.

It was about this time that Cert'nly Wilfred began his commissariat negotiations with the river Indians, negotiations which, unknowingly, were to exercise a profound influence upon us all. After we had anchored at night, and if there were Indians about, Wilfred, with one or two men in the launch, and armed with an odd assortment of articles to barter with, would go in search of a canoe and then give chase. To give chase was necessary and revealed in unmistakeable terms just how the Indians regarded white men and just how the alleged white men of the Amazon Valley regarded the Indians! Wilfred's companions upon these occasions were usually four in number; first of all was Twocents, then one of the engineers in charge of the launch engine, a very hefty young Californian known as "Rocks,"—an astonishingly vigorous, bounding youth,—and, of course, Stadger. Off they would go in the gloom, the little cook, tiller in hand, very much in command of the expedition in spite of the fact that any engineer ranked higher upon the ship's papers than he. But upon the absorbing subject of personality one could dwell at length — if space afforded. They would mark down a canoe that looked, in the distance, as though there had been good hunting and fishing for its owners, and then the chase would begin. Of course there were nights when there were no Indians.

The chase would end in a tragi-comedy. The Indians would fly for their lives as a matter of course, and would endeavour to dodge the launch, but as the launch bore down upon them they would surrender with abject faces and frenziedly offer their cargo of fish or turtle eggs or tapir or manatee meat as the price of their lives. And it would sometimes take quite a time and almost force before the Indians were able to realise that exchange, and not murder and robbery, was intended. Then, in a pitiful, dazed manner they would accept the brightly coloured calico, hand-axes, beads, and tobacco thrust upon them. But their state of terror, no less than their incredulous astonishment when they found that they were to receive something in return for their wares, made a profound impression upon us all, forecastle and after guard as well.

Gradually, in the wholly mysterious way in which news has of spreading up and down the

Amazon, it became known among the river Indians — even far ahead of us — that there was
a steamer flying a striped flag with stars on it
that *paid* for what the Indians had to offer in
the way of fresh food, and that this was even
so when dealing with, perhaps, an old Indian
woman and a girl who could have offered no
resistance anyway! But more than this became known; something infinitely subtle and
hard to describe; and Wilfred's expeditions in
search of fresh food became less difficult until,
finally, fresh food was offered for sale from
canoes that came alongside the ship as soon as
we had anchored at night.

Cert'nly Wilfred conducted his negotiations
not only in a strictly honourable manner, but
with a keen eye to getting his legitimate money's
worth on behalf of the ship, and — and here is
where the subtlety comes in — with a certain
affable and sympathetic understanding that had
yet the reserve of the dominating white man.
He did not treat the Indians as his equals; far
from it; he treated them as very much his inferiors, as, of course, they were; but he treated
them as inferiors who had rights and privileges,
ideas and customs entitled to all respect and
consideration — much, in fact, as he treated
Stadger, and had Wilfred died Stadger would
have died also. Wilfred was an Englishman,

and it is just this strange, instinctive ability which Englishmen possess that has made the British Empire an empire of four hundred million souls. All over the world men of all conditions, stations, and nationalities long for sympathetic understanding. Men often marry for no other reason, and it is the basis of all friendship. It is the keynote of real charity; it is the gift of the gods, the dominant force of real genius, the excellence of true judgment, and is, in short, divine. Could some superman, as greatly above the white man as the white man is above the Indian, offer the white man his sympathy and understanding, the white man would lie down and worship. So it was with the Indians. They became pathetically desirous of our notice, though just how the news concerning us was circulated was, as I have said, a mystery.

One evening as we anchored, there appeared, out of the shades of evening and the great shadow of the forest that was preparing for its nightly concert of strange sounds, a canoe laden with fresh fish, and among her people a man with a shockingly broken leg. Wilfred went down the ladder to do his bartering from the bottom grating, and after a moment or two we saw him push the canoe along and minutely examine an Indian lying in the bows, while the other occupants of the canoe, three women and two men, endeavoured to explain something which we, hanging over the side above, could not make out. Wilfred turned to us and called up that the Indian's leg was shattered and in an advanced gangrenous state, and that the Indians wanted us to attend to it. The cook added weight to his communication by an apt description of the injury which I will not repeat here, but which was, all the same, strictly accurate. Captain Hawks, with lanterns, and with Captain Esterkay as interpreter, went down to investigate, and I gathered from my commander's sudden, bark-like exclamation that Wilfred had not overstated the case, for Captain Matthew Hawks was not afflicted with a delicate stomach. He called me down. I went; and I was glad that I had had my dinner. The leg was rotting from the knee down, and I readily agreed that unless the leg was removed, and removed quickly, the Indian would have no chance of living another week. How it was that the Indian was still alive was a mystery. The man was a stoic of the first order, and he must have suffered the most shocking agony for days; but he and his friends and relations positively refused the captain's offer to rush the patient down to Obidos in the launch. In this they were backed up by Captain Esterkay.

"Besides the delay," said that excellent

Southerner, "there is no guarantee, suh, that a doctor will cut off his leg for him when he does arrive. Yo' see he's an Indian!"

"Then I'll cut it off for him," replied Captain Hawks briskly; for there was something infinitely moving in the attitude of these Indians, who had come to us in their trouble because we treated them as human beings and paid them for our fish and vegetables!

Captain Hawks ran up to the deck and into his cabin and returned with a hypodermic syringe, an instrument without which he never set out upon a lengthy voyage.

"I've got no use for pain, real pain," he used to say to me, "either for myself or for other people. I don't see what it's for." And more than once have I known that hypodermic of his bring ease to a poor human frame shattered and mauled by some sea accident. But it is an engine that must be kept under lock and key!

With complete trust the injured man submitted to what must have been a very strange proceeding to him, and in a very short time his attitude became more relaxed as the merciful peace stole over him and the great power of opium took him in charge. The memory of the change that took place in that Indian's expression will always remain vividly in my mind — it was magical. By this time the night had descended with its diabolic sounds from the forest. The entire ship's company was intent upon the business in hand; the ship herself was strangely quiet now that the engines had ceased, and was ringing metallically to every footfall.

"We have just got to go through with this, Grummet," said Captain Hawks privately to me, "though I'm not sure that I would n't rather face another full-dress typhoon. But there's no way out. It must be done and we are the only people to do it."

"Yes, sir," I nodded; and I confess that I was full of dread, for I knew that I must help.

"A white man," continued the captain, "would have been dead days ago, especially in this climate, with such an injury." Then, turning, he called the little cook. "Wilfred!" said he.

"Sir?" said Wilfred.

"Shift everything moveable out of the cabin. Get mosquito curtains ready to cover all doors, ports, and the skylights. Hump yourself!"

Wilfred vanished.

"Now," continued the captain to me, "who in this ship has the strongest stomach and the best nerve?"

"You, sir," I answered promptly.

"Quite so," admitted Captain Hawks simply; "but I must have at least three helpers and you have got to be one. Esterkay?"

I shook my head. "He has other virtues," said I, "and Hanks is a bit young. Mr. Mc-Lushley, sir, I should say has the stomach and the nerve of a steel bollard steeped in re-enforced concrete. And Wilfred, sir, though maybe he has a delicate stomach —"

"Wilfred's afraid of nothing on earth," chuckled the captain, "not even of me! Very good; then it'll be you, McLushley, Wilfred, and myself. Meanwhile get the patient aboard while I start on my preparations."

I arranged four lines over the side, passed them beneath the canoe, and by means of our extensive cargo tackle I swung the injured man aboard without a jar and without removing him from the canoe, which we placed in chocks upon the after main-deck. The Indian's friends and relations came up the ladder greatly excited and much entertained with everything. The patient himself lay passive and mute, free of pain and blinking slightly at the lights. He was clad in the dirtiest shirt I have ever seen, and what had once been his leg was retained and collected in a blanket. We had a hair-raising job removing that blanket, too! He put out his hand, and smiling slightly murmured, "Terbac," and at least a dozen well-filled pipes and as many cigarettes were instantly thrust at him. The only man in the ship who remained antipathetic was Mr. Alonzo Makepeace Massingbird. He displayed some contemptuous astonishment at our action, and was obviously puzzled to understand our motive.

"He's not your Indian, is he?" he enquired finally.

This question was overheard by some of the men and uncomplimentary mutterings answered him. Mr. Massingbird looked angry and I became uneasy. Our crew were excellent men, but meekness and gentleness were not their particular virtues. For two pins they would, then and there, have pitched Mr. Massingbird over the side to the alligators, and Mr. Massingbird, who was no kind of coward, glared back at them angrily.

"I think you are fools to bother over the Indian at all!" he remarked calmly; and right then I was prepared to fight for Mr. Massingbird's life, for as mate I represented law and order.

But Mr. McLushley, who was standing gaunt and sardonic among us, and who appeared equally unmoved either by the Indian's plight or Mr. Massingbird's remark, made answer, and the crew, knowing that something pretty nasty was thus guaranteed to come, remained quiet. I think that this was only the second time that the chief had addressed Mr. Massingbird; the first time had been to inform him that the engine-room was private and that "passengers werre no' admeetud."

"Mr. Massingwail," said the Scotchman with great clearness of utterance, "there was once a gr-rand Scotch poet that ye'll no' have heerd of called Robbie Burrns. An' Burrns, the eemorrtal, once said wi' th' wisdom o' the gods: —

> 'O wad some power the giftie gie us,
> To see oursels as ithers see us.'

It is a great peety, Mr. Massingale, ye have no' that geeft ye'self, though, creeation, man, it'd be an aufu' shock!"

I went forward to see how matters were progressing and found the cabin thick with smoke from a pan of burning disinfectants that cleared the place for once of all the countless insects that used the cabin as a sort of ballroom and meeting-house combined. Captain Hawks, in his cabin, was collecting basins of antiseptics and the instruments to be used in the coming event, and at the sight of his preparations my stomach turned over.

All shipmasters engaged in "blue-water" traffic are astonishingly handy with doctors' tools. They have to be, and it was in keeping with my commander's general character that he was more handy than most. In fact, while on this subject, I am tempted to paraphrase a well-known quotation as follows: —

"Oh, ye doctors in hospitals, who operate at ease,
  How little do you dream upon the dangers of the seas!"

But the amputation of a leg is a serious matter, though Captain Hawks could lop off a finger, pull a tooth, or put an arm in splints with any man. The captain moved with a steady deliberation. He was not going to forget anything.

"I would n't do it," said he, finally, to me, "if I thought that there was a chance of any one else doing it, or if I thought that there was a chance that the man would live if it was n't done. But, as far as I can see, the man will die unless I cut off his leg, — eh, Grummet?"

"That's undoubtedly so, sir," I answered, and he nodded.

"Very good; then I must cut off his leg, even if I kill him in doing it, — eh, Grummet?"

"Yes, sir. I see no alternative."

"Neither do I, but I wanted your assurance." And he continued with his methodical preparations in the same unhurried manner as though he had forced himself into a state of calm tranquillity.

As soon as the smoke cleared from the cabin and everything moveable was gone except the table, all the lights were turned on and a bunch of lights on an extension from the sleeping-cabins was arranged right over the table, and on the table itself was placed a tray of thin planking over which was drawn a sheet of rubber-silk. The whole place was sprayed and sprayed again with disinfectants until it reeked like a dozen hospitals. Captain Hawks, Mr. McLushley, Wilfred, and myself then bathed and put on clean pyjamas and were then ourselves sprayed with disinfectants until we choked. Mr. McLushley, Wilfred, and myself had our most precise instructions, and both the little cook and I were by no means happy.

"I wish it was this 'ere Messybird's leg wot we was goin' ter whittle orf, I do!" muttered Wilfred petulantly, and for the first time in all the years I have known him I saw fear in his expression.

Only Mr. McLushley appeared wholly unmoved, and his habitual expression of sardonic contempt for everything remained unaltered. But he trod as softly as a cat, with a swift alertness in all his movements.

Then the patient was brought into the heavily curtained cabin that was, for once, free of all insects. He was semi-comatose from his first dose of morphia, while his implicit trust in us greatly added to his chance of life. In fact, he alone among us appeared to enjoy complete ease of mind! The captain injected another dose of morphia while I washed, antiseptically, the leg and arranged the tourniquet, which, however, I did not screw up until the second dose of morphia had had time to work upon him. Wilfred, with compressed lips and a fiercely attentive expression, attended to the basins and the boiled bandages. Mr. McLushley stood by the Indian's head, with one eye upon the Indian and the other on the captain, or so it seemed, ready to anticipate any gesture. For me there was a worse — oh, far worse — job!

It was difficult with such a patient to know just how much and how little morphia to give, and we passed some awful moments watching the Indian's wide-open eyes as the pupils contracted to pin-points in size. So odd was his change of expression and so great our suspense that even Mr. McLushley was startled.

"Man!" said he, to the captain, though usually he addressed the captain with his full name and title, "I'm thinkin' he's deed. Yon morrphia's potent stuff. Na!" he added, with his battered fingers on the Indian's pulse, "he's alive so far."

We waited yet another moment to make sure.

"He'll do," said the captain; then glanced upward through the mosquito curtains at the skylight, where, with the exception of Mr. Massingbird's, were the collected heads of every man in the ship.

"Now, not a sound, up there," said Captain Hawks in a quiet voice, "or God help you when I get through with this."

His order was obeyed.

I tightened up the tourniquet; it was a silk scarf and a brass curtain rod. When I had finished all was ready.

Captain Hawks began, and whatever he might have felt, his large, powerful, capable hands were steady as a rock. No doubt doctors and nurses may laugh at us and consider that we cut sorry figures, but this was not our business, this business of amputating a leg, and the same doctors and nurses that laugh might cut no better figure did they try to navigate a ship.

The sawing was accomplished in six motions, and the sound of it bathed me in sweat. Wilfred snatched at that which was severed and stowed it out of sight, while the captain and I fell to work upon the arteries with linen thread. We were not sailors for nothing, and the knots we used were swift and sure. And once I fell actively to work, my nervousness left me. Naturally one was intent upon the job which done well would mean so much to another man. The worst was for Wilfred who had to stand by and hand things, and for Mr. McLushley who had to watch for any sign of returning consciousness in the patient, for remember that we had no proper anæsthetics. To find the small arteries we had to release a turn or two of the tourniquet; there was then no doubt where they were disposed! Then followed the kneading and pulling, and the angle of the cutting having been just right, the elastic flesh came handsomely (to use a sailor's expression) over the bone stump, and all the time the Indian never moved or made a sound. Then followed the stitches, the boiled bandages, and the lint. The last wrapping finished, drawn tight and true as though we had been serving the gear of a dandy sailing ship, and we carried the Indian upon the thin planking into a cabin and laid him in a bunk.

The operation was over, but, as the captain said, it remained to be seen if the patient lived.

We stood a moment dazed with the effort.

"Gee-mima!!" gasped Wilfred explosively; "I'm goin' ter be sick, I am, like a bloomin' sea-sick passenger!" And sick, indeed, was he.

But the patient lived!

CHAPTER VI

TROUBLE

WHEN a ship starts upon a voyage, for instance across the Atlantic, her people know, when they have dropped the land, that so many days and nights will elapse before the ship arrives at her destination. The mind accepts the situation and instinctively adjusts itself to the distance that it is necessary to cover to get across the ocean. In other words, you measure the distance in units of time. But in the navigation of rivers one has to become accustomed to measure distances, not in days, but in hours, and however long it may be, it will be but a trifle compared to the days and weeks at sea. By the above I do not mean the precise measurements necessitated by the exacting art of navigation, but the instinctive processes of the mind.

But in ascending the Amazon the ordinary order of things is reversed, and I was inclined to consider our run from Galveston to Para as the trifle, and that the real voyage began at Para. Of course, the distance up the river appeared greater on account of the nightly interruptions and by comparison with other rivers.

Before the days of steam, sailing vessels are reported to have taken five months to ascend from Para to the junction of the Rio Negro, and five months more to reach the Peruvian frontier. Beyond the Peruvian frontier the river continues for some fifteen hundred miles into the heart of the Andean regions through a series of wonderful gorges and over innumerable falls and rapids that are, for the most part, quite incorrectly charted. You will see from this that the Amazon is what might be called a good-sizeable river, and I therefore took some time before I could get out of the habit of peering ahead in expectation of seeing the forest give way to the buildings of man; to realise, in fact, that here man was but a trivial influence upon such primeval surroundings. He did not belong in such a place; he was out of scale. It was monotonously vast and never changing, smothered with vegetation, and always unbearably humid.

"I never don't want to see no tree again, I do," said Wilfred, with his usual involved cockney. "I'm not 'arf fed-up wiv trees, I ain't. I'd like to see a hiceberg. I'd like to sit on a hiceberg. I'd like to be frozen stiff hinside a hiceberg — like a sort of crystallised cook, fer that 'ere galley is sompthink chronic, with the stove goin' full, in this climate."

And, indeed, the only people in the ship who did not seem to mind the heat, the continuous, ever-present, damp, velvety heat, were the two Chinese stewards and Mr. Massingbird. The two stewards, lank, slim, and silent, each clothed in but two garments, did their work in a Chinese isolation that invited no Christian intrusion. And over these remote Orientals Wilfred held sway, minutely inspecting their work with the hawk-eye of a housewife, and with a ready tongue no housewife (I hope) ever possessed.

In our zigzag course up-stream we dodged acres of floating islands, and some of these were of such dimensions as to deceive the eye into believing them to be solid land until our wash set these tree-entangled masses visibly undulating. By day that ever-continuous, slightly varying wall of green; dark, indescribably sombre and silent, treacherous and mysterious; suggested some inscrutable Sphinx-like spirit that regarded us forebodingly with ill intent. The sense of remoteness took hold of us all, a feeling of loneliness and immeasurable distances. We were strange, foolhardy little creatures thrusting our way with vain temerity, and the spirit of the forest seemed to be watching us, as though we were going to our doom. We were going back, back, back in the ages of time, and it was not our surroundings that were extraordinary, but ourselves, with our compass, our steam power, our regular, cooked meals, and our concerted discipline. We should have been creeping about with a club torn from the nearest tree and with fear in our hearts, wholly intent upon the difficult problem of somehow keeping alive for the sake of the sheltered generations to come. Widely separated into warlike, unreasoning bands, we should, when not tracking down our dinner and eating it raw, or bellowing strangely at the strong scent of some unknown male, have been sleeping the cautious sleep of wild animals. Or, if awake and not hunting or eating, we might, perhaps, have been scratching our thoughts upon bone, making meanwhile the inarticulate noises that were the forerunners of man's eloquence. It seemed no wonder, I thought, that men deteriorated shockingly into savages and worse in such surroundings, and this brings me to the trouble with Mr. Alonzo Makepeace Massingbird.

The incident was an eye-opener to us, but was not so to Captain Esterkay, who knew well the region and the "white men" living in it. It was a most emphatic reminder that we, in our little sane and ordinary world composed by the ship and her company, were passing ever farther and farther into a strange and unknown surrounding that we could not hope to understand.

The difficulty came about over the negro carpenter.

I think that I have already referred to him. His name was no less than Andrew Jackson Jefferson Davis, and in most ways but one, Andrew was like any other rather tough old negro of the marine order. His one startling peculiarity was that he was dumb. He could make, when he chose, rather ghastly and partially comprehensible sounds; but articulate speech had gone from him one day with his tongue when he had brought upon himself the ferocity of some negro secret society in New Orleans.

Andrew was engaged in repairing the mosquito bar in Mr. Massingbird's cabin, and in doing so he upset a bottle of ink. In a blaze the real Massingbird showed himself, and the sight must have been particularly ugly. That Iberianated Amazonian had the usual and shocking attitude to men of colour, be they Indian or negro, that prevails throughout Amazonia. Now, my commander had no false notions concerning negroes; he did not regard them as equals as do those people who have never really come in contact with them, but the negro has his place in the order of things, a place which he must keep and where he has every right to be, and a skilled negro carpenter, sober, industrious, and honest, is entitled to just treatment and

respect. But Mr. Massingbird regarded all men
of colour as — well, I do not know just how he
regarded them; for, on entering his cabin and
beholding Andrew trying to mop up the ink
with a clean towel, he struck him a very violent
blow on the head — *from behind* — with the
butt of a six-shooter which he habitually carried about with him. Andrew, in spite of his
negroid skull, went down as though pole-axed.
It is difficult to say precisely what would then
have happened had not Cert'nly Wilfred happened by at the moment and to have observed
the blow. Possibly Mr. Massingbird intended
to use his feet to the prostrate negro. I do not
know. I do not understand those persons who
are engaged in the rubber industry of the Amazon, and I do not want to.

Wilfred stood stock still with sheer amaze
ment at the baseness of the action, and then, as
was the little man's habit on most occasions, he
opened his mouth in speech. He said just precisely what was in his mind — as was also his
habit — and what was in his mind was just
what would have been in any other decent man's
mind after witnessing such an action. I do not
expect that Mr. Massingbird understood one
word in ten of the little man's vitriolic cockney,
for, when really roused, words streamed from
Wilfred as water streams from a fire hydrant.

No man, not even a Latin, can beat the real cockney in wealth or diversity of epithet, and where the Latin is inclined to lose point by picturesque (artistic ?) exaggeration, there is a cutting aptness in the true Londoner's tirade that bites like an acid. Mr. Massingbird may not have grasped the detail, but he understood the general trend of Wilfred's remarks, and, in consequence, advanced upon the cook, sliding his revolver back into his pocket, for Wilfred was a white man and could not be shot down there and then.

Nothing could have pleased Wilfred more than Mr. Massingbird's advance, and according to the cook's account he " 'it that 'ere Messybird a smack in the starboard light," and Mr. Massingbird went backward over the still prostrate negro with his right eye swelling rapidly. Wilfred is a small man, but he can hit a smart blow, — I know that, for he once hit me and tried to go on hitting while I sat on him, — so Mr. Massingbird, unused to any form of rough-and-tumble, "saw red." At that moment Timothy Hanks, aroused by the considerable uproar, came out of his cabin and arrived upon the scene in a hurry. Taking in the situation at a glance, he ordered Wilfred out. In the face of such authority as the second mate, the little cook had, of course, to withdraw; but he withdrew slowly, remarking loudly upon Mr. Massingbird's past, present, and probable future, upon his probable origin and upon his personal appearance, in which he alluded in unmistakeable terms to the fact that Mr. Massingbird's finger-nails were tinted violet. He also entreated Mr. Massingbird to rise in order that he might have the great pleasure of knocking him down again. It is possible that Timothy Hanks, that grave young New Englander, considered that Mr. Massingbird deserved all he got, for he did not silence Wilfred, but, on the contrary, he stood listening and eyeing Mr. Massingbird with a sardonic grin. When, however, the little cook was forced to pause for breath, Timothy jerked his thumb over his shoulder, and, glancing at Wilfred, said, "Get," and Wilfred, partially appeased, and mistaking not the official order from a superior, departed.

By that time Mr. Massingbird had regained his feet and he was filled to the brim with puzzled rage. Timothy Hanks turned his attention to the carpenter, and quelling Andrew's natural desire for retaliation with a sharp order, he examined his head, and finding that the negro was not much the worse for the crack he had received, he told him to go and take a spell below.

Meanwhile, Mr. Massingbird had seated himself, with one hand to his eye. But it was not the pain of his eye that was absorbing Mr. Massingbird's thoughts, but the oddity of his surroundings. Very abruptly he had discovered himself in an unknown world, where, apparently, you must not hit even negroes from behind with the butt of a revolver — even when they spill a bottle of ink all over the prospectus of a rubber company as yet not actually in existence. Moreover, he, the director of many companies, had received a very sharp blow in the eye from a sea cook, — a menial, — and Timothy Hanks, the second mate, had not even hit the said sea cook in punishment. That a white man should take the part of a negro against him bewildered Mr. Massingbird. Then his bewilderment gave place to rage, and, brushing past Timothy Hanks, he went in search of Captain Hawks upon the bridge.

I was on the bridge at the time, and the captain and Captain Esterkay were playing chess, a game at which Captain Esterkay was a marvel. Therefore my commander was beaten nine times out of ten. But it so happened that upon that particular occasion, Captain Hawks was winning, and he had just remarked, "Mate Alexander, I've got you frazzled," when Wilfred arrived to report, with official regret, but with a grin on his face, that he had "bashed that 'ere Mister Messybird a clip in the peeper."

"What for? Why? When?" demanded Captain Hawks with a frown.

Wilfred explained the situation and the circumstances.

"All right, that will do," replied the captain; and the little man finished his speech, knuckled his forehead, kicked out his leg astern in true nautical fashion, wheeled about, winked at me, and departed. In his galley I could hear him singing: —

> "With a ladder and the glarses
> You could see the 'Ackney Marshes —
> If it wasn't fer the 'ouses in bertween. . . ."

"This is serious," said Captain Esterkay, rising.

"It is," agreed Captain Hawks. "I don't allow passengers to knock my crew about, and I am delighted that Wilfred punched him."

"That's not what I mean!" gasped Captain Esterkay. "Say, Matthew, yo' just don't know where yo' are! Massingbird is —" And at that moment Mr. Massingbird arrived.

In the short distance between his cabin and the bridge, Mr. Massingbird's anger had risen to an extraordinary pitch. Such maniacal anger is seldom known in more temperate climes; it is a product of fevers, of nerves shattered and abused, and of the lack of healthy exercise. Mr. Massingbird arrived two steps at a time, and there were bubbles upon his lips. Now, usually, a man in a rage is one of three things. Either he is dangerous, or impressive, or he is just ridiculous according to the kind of man that he happens to be. Mr. Massingbird was dangerous. He was so angry that, for the moment, he was not sane, and he had an automatic pistol in his pocket.

Captain Hawks at once began to apologise for the conduct of his cook. It was not, I must admit, an apology very heartily given; but it was an official apology, nevertheless, and Mr. Massingbird was assured that the cook would be logged for gross insubordination.

"But I must ask you, Mr. Massingbird," concluded Captain Hawks, "to report any incident to me in which my men have behaved carelessly, when I or my mate will handle the — er — situation. In other words, we are quite capable of bashing a man if such should be necessary. Still, it was no business of my cook's to interfere, and I hope that you will accept my apology."

Mr. Massingbird did not accept the apology; he foamed at the mouth instead, and in his insane behaviour I saw, for the first time, what we, in the *Martin Connor* termed "Amazonitis." In other words, I saw, for the first time, the effect of a prolonged residence in the Upper

Amazon country upon a man when that man gets angry. Mr. Massingbird, to all intents and purposes, went temporarily mad. He was not at all ridiculous in his madness, as a man may be when mad with rage in our sane and ordinary world. His rage was startling and horrible, and was a direct and lucid explanation of how it is that the things that happen among the rubber dealers in the Upper Amazon come to pass. I understand that in some parts of the Congo you will also find "Amazonitis," and from just the same causes. That which controls us, and which prevents us, even in the worst moods, from doing certain things, becomes wilted and destroyed in such a place and climate. As a man in a passion may slam a door, a man in a passion in the Amazon Valley will shoot another, preferably an Indian.

Mr. Massingbird whipped out a revolver and levelled it at my commander with a trembling hand!

I happened to be nearest him, and as he pulled the trigger I hit him squarely beneath the ear. It was a hard blow, but the time was not one for nice discrimination, and Mr. Massingbird dropped in a heap.

"The sarpentile insect!" exclaimed Captain Esterkay, for the bullet had narrowly missed him, having passed between him and Captain

Hawks. For a moment we stood astonished, with Mr. Massingbird lying tragically insignificant like a bundle of white clothes. Then the same thought occurred to us all three, for there was something odd in Mr. Massingbird's attitude, and in a panic we leaned over the prostrate man.

Mr. Alonzo Makepeace Massingbird was dead!

The deck seemed to take a half-turn under me at the discovery, then righted itself; yet I had the vivid sensation of having passed through a doorway through which there was no return. Mr. Massingbird was dead and I had killed him. He, a moment before, had been a living thing with thoughts and aspirations, temporarily clouded, it is true, with what amounted to homicidal mania; yet he had been a man, a separate entity, a creature capable of independent action good or bad. And now he was a pathetic, small, crumpled pile of white clothing, with feet turned inwards, the upturned soles exposing a hole in his left shoe, while a wrist-watch still ticked on his brown left wrist. It was the biggest and most horrible shock I have ever had in my life, for there was a sense of blind, helpless impotency, as though I had been forced into a cruelly false position. And there was, amidst all the tragedy, an appalling futility. A man was dead; another man had killed him because a third man had spilled a bottle of ink!

At that moment Captain Hawks demonstrated just why he was in command of a ship. He stood up, put a whistle in his mouth, and brought the boatswain and two men aft.

"Mr. Massingbird is dead," said he, to 'Arry Ketchold, as though issuing an ordinary sea order; "help me to carry him to his cabin below."

At the report of Mr. Massingbird's revolver shot, an expectant shudder had gone through the ship. They had heard it even in the engine-room, and then a quietness fell upon the ship which continued its uninterrupted journey as the forest continued, as the river continued, unchanged, yet suddenly changed for me. The man at the wheel, who had seen it all, had never moved the ship one foot off her course, and his eyes again rested upon the spot last pointed out to him by Captain Esterkay, beneath which he unswervingly kept our iron bows. And then the thought possessed me that, considering the state that Mr. Massingbird had been in, there had been little chance of his hitting any one and that I had probably killed him for nothing. There was, of course, his intention to kill. But should a man be killed under such conditions?

Captain Hawks returned to the bridge and

put his hand upon my shoulder. "You did it to save my life, Grummet," said he.

"I did, sir," I replied, "but —"

"No 'buts' about it, Grummet. If he had n't been as rotten as an egg he would n't have died."

"You — you examined him, sir?"

The captain nodded grimly. "Neck snapped like a carrot."

"He should n't have been so brittle, suh," remarked Captain Esterkay in his suave voice as smooth as velvet. "And to hit the animal —"

"Hush, he's dead!" I cried.

"He's no more respectable dead than alive, suh," replied the Southerner politely and with wisdom. "To hit him was the most reasonable thing to do under the circumstances."

"I'll go down to my cabin, sir," said I to the captain, and he nodded and smiled.

"Don't you get jumpy and leery, now," said he, as I left the bridge.

I cannot give an exact description of the hours that followed Massingbird's death, yet certain more or less trivial impressions will always remain in my memory. Chief among these is the picture of Massingbird's cabin door, shut and locked by the captain upon the mortal remains of that unhappy man. While I yet regarded that varnished teak door with its white china doorknob, Wilfred appeared silently at my side.

"YOU DID IT TO SAVE MY LIFE"

" 'E's dead, pore bloke," remarked the little cook in a matter-of-fact voice, as though referring to the weather; " 'e did n't ought to 'ave been so 'asty wiv 'is gun, 'e did n't, butt end or business end. But 'e'll learn better by 'nd by, like most of us, but 'e 'as an awful long way to go! And if I could do anythink for 'im now, I'd do it, seein' as 'ow bygones is bygones. But maybe they'll learn 'im quicker wheer 'e's gorn to than wot 'e learned 'ere. Leastways, that's 'ow it seems to me. So don't you feel bad about it, Grummet. You could n't 'ave done less than what you did do, hunder the circumstances."

What precisely would be the results of my action I did not know. Captain Hawks wrote out the matter in the log and Captain Esterkay and the man at the wheel signed it as being a true and impartial statement; and all the time the ship's business continued, as life continues, no matter what happens.

It was necessary, however, since we were not at sea, to communicate with some form of authority ashore, and that as soon as possible. Massingbird had been a person of importance, and, though we did not know it at the time, had been practically a spy in the pay of the Rio Maranon Rubber Company, which company was none too friendlily inclined to us at any time. And, to put it definitely, we were a very long way—much farther than the actual distance in miles — from the United States of North America. There seemed to be an evil genius at work. Looking back I marvel at the strange perversity of the fate that never left us during that portion of the cruise, when everything should have been in our favour, but which left us as suddenly when, according to the "doctrine of probabilities," we should have been slaughtered to a man.

The Government of Brazil is divided and subdivided and divided yet again into departments, sections, and districts; and to the less-favoured districts go the less-favoured governors, and the worst of all, districts and governors, are found in the Upper Amazon country. Here, in the very home of the Rio Maranon Company, any official who wishes to remain alive will work hand in hand with the company that practically owns a stretch of country more than a quarter the size of the United States. At Para there is an American Consul, but at Manaos there was — when we were there — an American Agent who was a Brazilian; a fat man who knew just upon which side his bread was buttered; and it is enough to say that he knew that it was not buttered on the American side! At Manaos there was also a British Agent; an Englishman with a chequered career, a "hobnailed" liver,

and a very great knowledge of Brazilian officials in the Upper Amazon, and a still greater
knowledge of the Rio Maranon Company. He
had, that British Agent with the liver (so we
learned later), written out a very lucid description of the character and actions of the Rio
Maranon Rubber Company and had mailed a
copy to the British Foreign Office in London.
His account had concluded with the gentle hint
that if his death should occur, no matter how
reported, the circumstances of his exit should
be enquired into by his own Government; and
his own Government had replied, thanking him
for the document, which would be kept for possible use in the future and assuring him that
all details concerning his death, if such an event
were to take place, would be enquired into at
once by the commanding officer of the nearest British man-o'-war. The British Agent had
then sent a copy of the entire correspondence,
including his own report, to the Rio Maranon
Company. The net result of this action had
been that the British Agent at Manaos went
where he pleased, said what he pleased, and did
what he pleased.

To the Brazilian American Agent at Manaos,
Captain Hawks made his report concerning
Massingbird's death, and sought advice. The
Brazilian was friendly in the extreme and ar-

ranged to receive the remains of Mr. Massingbird. He also gave my commander instructions
as to where to go and whom to see; and it was
to be arranged (with much waving of hands
and many high-sounding phrases) that Captain
Hawks, Captain Esterkay, the man at the wheel,
and myself should appear before some form of
local magistracy the following day, when only a
formal matter of enquiry should be made — or
so said the Brazilian. My commander came
away from his interview very much worried and
puzzled. It was, apparently, the most usual
thing in the world to hit a man under the ear
and kill him. The matter seemed simple enough,
and the more that the captain thought of it the
more he became convinced that it was altogether
too simple, or that it sounded too simple. And
then he had an inspiration. He went to see the
British Agent — just for advice.

Now, an American and an Englishman may
be two very different men, belonging to two
very different nations when in New York or London, but there is remarkably little difference
between them when they meet in the wilds of a
country foreign to them both. My commander
and the British Agent evidently got along splendidly together, and when Captain Hawks came
away he was no longer puzzled — but he was in
a hurry. For the advice he had received was

simple and to the point. It was: "Send the gentleman, who died suddenly, ashore to our friend the Brazilian, just as he said. Give me a written copy of your account in the log book, which I will transmit to your American Consul at Para (nice fellah, known him for years), and get out of this up-stream. Don't attend any court here or elsewhere except at Para, and be careful who you let on board your ship from now on!"

It may seem strange that Captain Hawks should take the advice of the representative of a foreign country in place of the advice given him by the representative of his own; but the circumstances were peculiar, as were the representatives in question. Moreover, my commander and the British Agent spoke the same language (or nearly so), and, with the exception of a few minor details, their ideas, their thoughts, and their lives revolved upon the same fundamental principles. In short, they understood each other. From the British Agent, also, Captain Hawks heard the first definite news of Colonel Ezra Calvin.

That evening we were proceeding full speed up-stream, taking advantage of a bright moon to continue under weigh throughout the night!

CHAPTER VII

THE COMPLETE ANGLERS

In one instant our voyage, which had been an ordinary, humdrum, commercial affair, seemed to have changed into something very different, and our departure from Manaos amounted to little more than flight.

"I guess that British Agent knew what he was talking about, Grummet," said Captain Hawks to me, as the ship made her way over a river of black and silver, while the forest stood like an ebony silhouette on the port side. "I have sent the statement to the American Consul at Para, telling him when we shall probably be back in Para, and asking him to make the necessary arrangements for me. At present we are buried at the back of beyond, and we are about as far from Rio as New Orleans is from San Francisco, and I guess that any politician who finds a change of air wholesome for his political health applies for a job somewhere west of Obidos."

"Just so, sir," I answered; "and we'd be in a nice fix if they really got a hold on us up here."

"That's what the British Agent said. He showed me conclusively that this country up

here don't belong to Brazil, but to the Rio Maranon Company. And the very least that they
would do, if they had the chance, would be to
hang the ship up indefinitely on some techni-
cality by putting you or me or both of us in jail;
and I don't hanker any after an up-country
jail in these parts. But as long as we stay by the
ship I don't see what they can do, for it is not
Brazil we are dealing with, but this pesky Rubber Trust."

"I understand that the Rio Maranon people
have a private army of their own," I began.

"They have," answered my commander
grimly; "some few hundred men and one or two
shallow-draught steamboats with a gun or two.
But are we such chickens?"

"No, sir; but if it comes to an out-and-out
scrap with them, what will Brazil say?"

"Brazil will say" — joined in Captain Esterkay amiably, — "will say to the Rio Maranon
Company: 'I wisht yo' would manage yo' little
troubles quieter. Yo' will mix us up with the
United States if yo' ain't careful!' But that is
all they will say, and the Rio Maranon Company will take the hint and try and kill us
quietly in the dark. But this is a big country.
There are many miles of it that neither Brazil
nor the Rio Maranon know anything about. We
are a needle in a haystack, Matthew, though

I expect that there will be trouble somewhere for some one before long."

"What did you hear of Colonel Calvin, sir?" I asked; and Captain Hawks laughed.

"He's in trouble too!" he answered. "The Rio Maranon found him prospecting for rubber and told him to get off the earth. He's still on the earth, and he replied by hammering one of the Rio Maranon officials with a tin dipper, and he has had to take to the woods!" And the captain flung out an expressive arm toward the forest!

"What d' yo' mean, Matthew?" asked Captain Esterkay quickly.

"What I say," replied my commander. "Calvin arrived at Para about eighteen months ago, hired a wood-burning steamer and started up-stream. He did n't ask permission, — why should he? I guess this river's big enough for every one, ain't it? He had his first tilt with the Rio Maranon at Serpa. They wanted to know all about him, and he, an American citizen, did n't see any necessity to publish an autobiography and said so; whereupon I gathered that there was trouble, for that is where he rubbed the fear of death into the Rio Maranon official with the tin dipper. He showed up next at Manaos, flapping the Stars and Stripes in the face of every one, and there ran across our

British Agent, who, I guess, was mighty glad to
see a white man between steamer times, for they
seem to have been friends on sight. That rather
put a check on the Rio Maranon Company,
for the British Agent swore blind that Calvin
was a friend of his childhood, that they had
stolen apples together, and that any inconven-
ience which his life-long friend suffered was
therefore a slight to him, — the British Agent,
who had never seen Calvin before in his life, —
and as there was a British Dreadnought coming
up-stream fishing for turtles' eggs, they had
better turn kind. Well, that saw Calvin out of
Manaos all right, but a day's run up the river
saw him in No-Man's-Land, or rather, in the
Rio Maranon Company's land, and a launch
overtook him and demanded his papers. They
told him pretty plain (so the British Agent
thought) that he was a poacher poaching rubber, and that he'd better go home. The crew of
the river boat which Calvin had hired were n't
going to put up a scrap naturally; so it was my
partner against every one, and I guess that he
had a lively time. He had no intention of being
arrested, knowing what that would mean, so he
took the wheel of his river boat and ran the Rio
Maranon launch under and laughed at 'em as
they scrambled ashore."

"Good man!" said I.

"He is a good man," continued the captain, "but he's not a wise one. He was now a recognised belligerent, and the crew of his river boat mutinied. They said — and I see their point — that the trouble was none of their making, and that, please, they would like to get back to Para. Well, Calvin quelled their desires, and however much they may have been scared of the Rio Maranon Company, Calvin so fixed it that they were still more scared of him. But he seems to have got on well with the river Indians, same as we have done; for the Indians smuggled letters for him through to our British friend at Manaos, who said, by the by, that Calvin's letters were most entertaining. In this way Calvin sent his letters to me at home, the British Agent giving them privately to the skipper of one of the Liverpool boats to post in Para. In the last of these he said that he was liable to find himself in serious trouble. Serious trouble! Why, he was then, at the time of writing, practically an outlaw, with the crew of his river boat ready to murder him if they got a chance. Meanwhile, he was getting to know a whole heap about the country, and had discovered, 'way, 'way off, a regular forest of the finest kind of rubber, situated in a patch of country claimed by Peru, by Colombia, by Ecuador, by Brazil, and by the Rio Maranon Company. He also discovered a river about the size of the Ohio at Cincinnati that is n't on the map."

"He seems to have been busy," breathed Captain Esterkay.

"He has been," replied Captain Hawks; "he usually is busy, but by this time his exploits had sifted down-stream to the local headquarters of the Rio Maranon Company which now made a real effort to bottle him. They sent out a river steamer with forty men, so our friend in Manaos told me, with instructions to bring Calvin back alive or dead; but preferably dead, for there was a rumour floating round that he was inciting the Indians to revolt against the tyranny of the rubber dealers. Well, they found him, 'way beyond the back of everything, and there was no doubt that this time the Rio Maranon Company meant business. So he quietly slipped ashore with some dunnage, and he has been lost in the jungle for six months!"

Captain Esterkay whistled long and emphatically.

"Then he is dead, Matthew," he pronounced softly; "*requiescat in pace!*"

"No more dead than you are," replied Captain Hawks. "You don't know Ezra Calvin; he comes from New England."

"I know the up-river country, though," said Captain Esterkay with the quiet assurance which knowledge gives; "that is where the Blow-gun Indians are, and no one, not even the Rio Maranon, can do anything against them and their blowguns. The blowgun, Matthew, makes a Winchester rifle look foolish; and in the hands of an expert it is the most deadly weapon in the world at a short range. The Indians that use it are stark naked heathen that just laugh at fire-arms, and no wonder!"

"Well, that's where Calvin is, and, when I have discharged my cargo at the Rio Maloca set-tlement, that is where I am going to find him."

Work is a great soother of troubled times. In three days the steady influence of discipline had lessened my constant and all-pervading memory of Massingbird's death, though I would come back to the recollection with a horrible shock. But a ship demands of her mate continual and active examination; one can be continually busy, and do no more than is necessary.

Whatever effect our sudden departure from Manaos may have had in that place, we trav-elled too far and too quickly for the news to overtake us in any official form. We were, in-deed, getting into the heart of the wilds, and beyond a very occasional Indian canoe we saw no sign of man for days. But even here the Indian form of wireless telegraphy had preceded us, and we had as much fresh food as we wished.

Our patient, whose leg we had amputated, had been removed to the forecastle, and his chilled-steel constitution was manifesting itself in the healthy way in which he healed. His Indian name was unpronounceable, but it sounded something like "Maryjane," so Maryjane he became, thenceforth and always. He was carried out daily and he sat in the shade smoking ship's tobacco and thus gradually assumed his place in our lives, as Stadger had done, and we should have missed him had he not been there. For he was what one might call an effective person in his way; he had character, and he made miraculous carvings for us all and wept tears of pure emotion to the music of the forecastle accordion. Thus Maryjane became a fixture.

The river was now distinctly narrower, or rather, its average was so; and by the narrowing of the river we came into more intimate touch with the forest. Moreover, the land, for the most part, was lying at a slightly higher level and there was frequently quite a high bank. The river had become a river as we know it, and though the forest remained as thick as ever it was not such a primeval swamp. The wealth of detail confused the eye, the shapes and shades of green distracted the attention, yet the country was assuming a more reasonable, a more realisable form. Once Captain Esterkay got us aground, and I spent a happy morning handling kedges and warps; I say "happy," for my efforts were successful, and any sailor will recognise what I mean when I speak of the strange exhilaration in dealing with powerful forces and immense weights.

The rain squalls in this upper country were excessively violent. The pearl-grey water came sluicing down in such tremendous volumes as to threaten the awnings that covered the ship. The rainfall was accompanied by a roaring sound like that heard when standing under an iron railroad bridge when a train passes overhead. But, for the most part, during the daytime there was a silence like deafness, broken only by the welcome noises of the ship.

There was a marked increase in the number of alligators, and the forest sounds at night were louder and more insistent. Strips of sandy beach would sometimes line the bank, and upon these were invariably to be seen one or more alligators — or crocodiles, we did not know which — looking for all the world like tree-trunks. Wilfred was devising an angling apparatus for catching one of these saurian monstrosities; and he gave forth the astonishing information that an alligator's eye-teeth, when ground to powder and applied as a hot compress, were

an infallible cure for rheumatism; whereat Mr.
McLushley affirmed that an alligator's eye-
teeth, when not ground to powder but in full
working order, were an infallible cure for all the
ills that man is heir to. In speaking of these
creatures do not think that I mean anything
like the caymans of Florida. The Amazon edition is in strict proportion with the size and
ferocity of the country, and once hooked would
need a steam winch and a wire warp to shift
him. They were the most repulsive-looking
objects, and they existed in such swarms as to
make the river bank a place of great danger.
The Indians, with whom we were in frequent contact, went in continual dread of the monsters,
which, according to them, knew no fear. It was
their fearless reputation, I think, that inspired
Wilfred with his idea. For it was not the little cook's intention to kill an alligator; he pro-
posed to capture one alive and take it home with
us in a cage on deck. The scheme was ambitious.

"D' you want one as a sort of pet, d' you
mean?" enquired Captain Hawks with a grin.

The captain and Wilfred and myself happened to be alone on the bridge, so we dropped
back to the familiar attitude toward one another
born of many long years of friendship.

"Well, I don't s'pose I'll be able to lead 'im
round wiv a string like a Fido dorg," said Wil-

fred, "but we could fix 'im up in a cage on the harfter main-deck — oncet we'd got 'im."

"And how d' you mean to get him?" asked Captain Hawks, — "put salt on his tail or just whistle?"

"You let me 'ave the use of a few men, a boat, one of them theer arfter shore-lines and a winch and *Hi* will get 'im aboard," answered Wilfred, with emphasis.

"All right, I will," replied the captain, "just to see how you will do it!" And he grinned down at the little Englishman with the affection of long intimacy.

As a matter of fact, my commander's reasons for giving his permission were threefold. He wanted to oblige Wilfred, for whom he entertained a sincere respect; he wanted, out of curiosity, to see how Wilfred would manage it; and none knew better than he the necessity for some recreation among a community of hard-working men penned up in a ship in a murderous climate.

So a cage capable of retaining a mad elephant was forthwith constructed upon the after main-deck by the carpenter and 'Arry Ketchold, Wilfred giving shrill advice. Then a running noose was fashioned in a stout manila line which, in turn, was bent to a short strip composed of a hundred strands of the best hemp cord, not twisted together, but placed in juxtaposition,

and bound at intervals of a few feet. These thin
lines would thus — so it was thought — slip
between the alligator's teeth when he tried to
bite the line. The thin lines in turn were bent
to a ring to which was made fast the sister-hooks
at the end of a long wire cable running to one
of the cargo derricks. The appliance was sailor-
like and efficient and would have lifted fifty
alligators once it was attached to them.

The affair was strictly Wilfred's. He was in
command of the operation, and the entire ship
trembled with excited expectation. There was
no difficulty in finding an alligator; the difficulty
was, once we started, to prevent the alligator
finding us. Within a hundred yards of the ship
at anchor was a sandbank upon which four large
alligators lay prone and half regarding us with
the unfearing insolence of savage wild animals
that have only regarded the infrequent men
they have encountered as possible food and
not as worthy enemies; for the Indians had
no weapons capable of really dealing with such
creatures. This, of course, does not refer to the
Blowgun Indians; but we were many miles from
the Blowgun Indians' country.

A boat put off quietly from the ship containing Wilfred in the bows, in command, and with
his lariat paid out astern alongside the boat and
attached by the sister-hooks to the wire, the

weight and pull of the latter being taken without effort by 'Arry Ketchold. Timothy Hanks
steered, while I stood by Wilfred's side with a
rifle for defensive purposes in case anything
miscarried. Softly and slowly we drifted down
to the alligators, Wilfred signing his commands
to the gravely smiling Timothy Hanks. He
picked out one that was reposing, or rather just
awakening, some forty yards from the others,
and which was lying at an angle, thus allowing
us to approach and avoid his tail as much as
possible. Hardly a man in the boat drew breath,
and the four men at the oars were ready to go
full astern with all the strength of eight muscular arms. We came so silently and so imperceptibly that the alligator either did not see, or did
not consider us worthy of his attention; for it
must be recollected that in that game-swarming
country man is at a discount. Suddenly, however, the alligator realised how close we were,
and the large ship's boat may have appeared
suddenly formidable to him then, for he whisked
round amid a great upheaval of sand and water
and presented an open mouth that was a shock
to behold. Then he came for us.

"Full astern and 'ard a-port!" yelled Wilfred,
and the boat slid round. " 'Old 'er!" he added
in a screech of delighted excitement.

The alligator was now within three feet of our

bows, but our sudden change of position disconcerted him, and he snapped together his gigantic jaws with a crack like the shutting of steel doors. It was at that precise moment that Wilfred positively *drew* — not threw — the noose over the beast's head, and he would have toppled over had I not dropped my rifle and snatched him back by the slack of his patched pants. As he fell back into the boat he clapped the whistle to his mouth and blew, while I yelled to our men to go astern for all our lives.

The boat shot backwards, and the waiting donkeyman on board the ship had started his winch the very second the whistle sounded, and the line came tight round the alligator's neck and just abaft the eight great lumps he carries there for some mysterious purpose of his own.

He was both an astonished and a very angry alligator, and to put it precisely, we had to get out of the way. If you have ever seen a really large alligator really angry and thoroughly surprised, you will appreciate what I say when I explain that we literally fled to the ship while the most extraordinary commotion commenced in the water. If you can imagine a torpedo miraculously imbued with intelligence and filled with appalled and devastating rage, you will imagine a little of what we saw. The river Ama-

zon was not half big enough for that alligator.
He went for the sandbank and the wire brought
him up with what must have been a nasty jar,
and the winch drawing him backwards raised
him high on his after legs for a moment. Then
he cast himself sideways, like a falling tree, and
quite illogically he went for his friends. But
again the wire brought him up sharp, and the
slack being now gathered in, he was drawn with
a sudden jerk off the sandbank and into the
river toward the ship. He darted up-stream,
then down-stream, and in a sudden mania of
rage fell to rolling round and round snapping
powerfully at the rope. But he could get no hold
on the hundred strands of twine, and whatever
he did the inexorable winch drew him swiftly
to the ship.

Meanwhile the evening air was filled with the
yells, shouts, and whistles of every man present,
punctuated by the heavy reports of the alligator's tail hitting the water. Provided that the
noose held and did not slip, he was ours, or
rather Wilfred's, and Wilfred whooped and
coughed, and cackled and crowed and danced
in the bows of our boat. As the inevitable wire
drew the alligator, rolling and plunging and
lashing, to the ship, our excitement grew positively painful. Then, for an indescribable space
of time, the alligator was in the air, rising sky-

wards, and doubling and twisting in a manner
that made him fearful to behold. The derrick
came clanking round with the same blind precision that would have marked its exact action
had the alligator been a grand piano or half a
ton of hay; and with the skilled neatness of long
practice the donkeyman deposited that raging
alligator in the roofless cage which had been
prepared for its reception.

We, in the boat, went aboard like monkeys,
and every man in the ship crowded round the
cage, while a man poised above unshackled
the sister-hooks and endeavoured to disengage
the noose from the reptile below him. Our captive had not too much room, but we had given
him as much space as we could afford, and he
filled that space completely and almost simultaneously in mad rushes to get at us, snapping
his terrific jaws and pounding the iron deck with
his prodigious after parts in great ringing thuds.
He did not know what fear was, that alligator;
and the trying experience he had just gone
through and the surrounding number of his enemies in no way dismayed him.

Wilfred went dancing round, butting into all
indiscriminately, extolling the virtues and beau-
ties of his pet in the high shrill whoops of great
exhilaration. He flung a large lump of pork into
the cage, but the alligator was not looking for

food; his spirit and his body demanded red revenge; and his implacable, unconquerable ferocity gained, not only our respect, but almost our affection. All through the night the alligator snapped his jaws and refused even to look at food that was offered him. On one side of the cage was a wooden trough just deep enough for him to lie in, while a short strip of hose from a deck hydrant enabled Wilfred to keep his pet in a healthy state of dampness. The reptile was, of course, a great source of interest to us all, and its refusal to take food at first caused much anxiety throughout the ship, and a genuine sigh of relief went up when Wilfred announced, two days later: "Percy is able to sit up and take a little nourishment. 'E's eat sixty-two pounds of fresh manatee!"

"We are coming on," said Captain Hawks to me. "We gathered in a dog at Para, then an Indian minus one leg, and now a very well-equipped alligator — or crocodile; don't know which. We should be a full ship's company by the end of the cruise at this rate."

Otherwise our journey continued as before, only with the difference that we were, as Captain Esterkay pointed out, minus a Massingbird and plus an alligator. But by now the river was noticeably smaller, while there had come a subtle difference in the forest that is hard to define.

There was the same interwoven jam of strenuous growth, but there were occasional stretches of forest that was forest as we know it in more civilised lands; great tall trees standing straight from solid earth, and not amid a matted tangle of half-aquatic growth. One day Captain Esterkay "shot the sun." This, in itself, seemed remarkable, and impressed me with the magnitude of our surroundings, especially as he found the best map procurable in the United States eleven miles in error!

A day later there was much excitement, for we left the main stream and turned into a southern tributary, and the navigation of the ship now became a matter of considerable care. Heretofore there had been so much river and so little ship that we had been able to take rather "easy" courses from far distant points, but we must now keep to the centre of the stream in all its windings, and the stream resembled a roadway through the forest that now seemed to close in on us as a tunnel closes upon a train. A marked change also came in the country, for occasionally, above the trees, we beheld rolling hills. At night we seemed to be actually in the forest, which echoed continually with strange cries of abundant life. Tributaries of the tributary we were in branched off at infrequent intervals, and few of these were marked upon the map.

Occasional bouts of fever visited us all, and one day, when Captain Hawks was groaning and shivering in his bunk, a turn in the river revealed a shallow - draught steamer coming down-stream and flying the flag of the Rio Maloca Rubber Company. We instantly greeted each other with prolonged whistles, and as I was in temporary command of the ship, I moved as much to one side as Captain Esterkay would let me and rang off the engines, sending Timothy Hanks onto the forecastle-head to be ready to let go the anchor; for of all things I hate it is the navigation of rivers in a seagoing ship.

"This will be Eichholz," said Captain Esterkay, with the glasses to his eyes; and Eichholz it was.

Our interest was as great as though we had met a ship at sea upon a long and lonely voyage, and every man who could do so crowded the deck. The broad-beamed, waddling steamer, spreading behind her a cloud of blue wood smoke, came sidling athwart the current. She lay upon the water like a dish, and as she was now obviously aiming for our side I regarded her manœuvres with growing alarm. I rang down the telegraph to "Stand by," and comforted myself with the knowledge of Mr. McLushley's always immediate responses. Along came that river boat full speed, swinging merrily from side to side as though undecided just where to ram us, while emphatic criticisms were flung at her from our decks.

"Fenders over the side!" I yelled, and rang on, "Slow astern."

The crew jumped, and not only fenders went over the side, but a six-inch manila — a sudden and excellent inspiration of Timothy Hanks's. And as the men jumped, they addressed the river boat in forceful United States, asking her to "Come right inside and not to be bashful"; to "Keep off the grass"; to "Ask mother to come and help"; and to "Part her hair in the middle."

"That'll do," said I; "shut your faces."

On the upper deck of the river steamer, congregated round a shed-like wheel-house and beneath a dirty, slack-stretched awning, lounged half a dozen alleged white men with the weariness and extraordinary languor marking their postures which seemed habitual with all men we had seen in the Amazon country. What these very dilapidated specimens thought of our vociferating, almost naked, truculently cheerful crew, swarming about us like apes, I do not know.

The visitor came alongside with a creaking, thumping jar that made the men by the wheelhouse stagger, and a raucous cackle of derisive merriment came from where Wilfred observed events from abaft the galley.

"Wheer did you get that 'at?" demanded the little man of a stooping individual on the river boat who wore a home-made arrangement on his head that was certainly remarkable.

"Go astern, sir!" I shouted to the man in the wheel-house, as his craft went sliding and thumping along our side like a travelling battering-ram; "go astern hard! If you have no paint, we have! Mr. Hanks! Heave that deaf, blind, paralytic idiot a line, and some of you there get over and make it fast. Jump!"

Six of our swarthy crew dropped down into the river boat with the end of a line, to the considerable consternation of the "niggers" and Indians and goodness-knows-whats upon her upper deck who were swept aside in the frenzied efforts which our men made to find something to which they could make fast.

"She ain't got no bollards, sir!" howled 'Arry Ketchold, and to try and stop the murderous bumping, he clutched the manila line in one terrific fist and hooked the other arm through a window of the wheel-house. The window frame and part of the wheel-house came away with a rending of wood and a tinkling of glass, while Wilfred cheered gleefully at the wreckage.

"Nothink like destruction!" he yelled; "I

loves ter see it! Parse the line round 'er skipper's perishin' neck, 'Arry, 'im with the 'at! Oh, I 'ave n't larfed so much since father died!"

At length our men found an anchorage by circumnavigating the deckhouse; and thus, by tying up the river boat as though she had been a parcel, they brought her to rest.

There was one man amid those standing round beneath the awning who had shown neither interest nor alarm during these proceedings, but who had regarded us without a vestige of animation. He was the man with the remarkable hat, and he came aboard us first and introduced himself to me.

"My name is Eichholz," said he, gazing wearily past me at nothing in particular; "are you Captain Hawks?"

As my commander's representative, I did the polite, and after ordering Timothy Hanks to let go the hook, I explained that the captain was down with a bout of fever.

"Jus' so," answered Eichholz, understandingly, and took the chair I offered.

Eichholz I have placed permanently among my gallery of human curiosities. He was incredibly thin and unusually tall. He moved, spoke, and even seemed to breathe with calculated deliberation and with occasional lapses of consciousness, as though he forgot to live.

Extreme caution marked his most trivial action, while he possessed an odd mannerism that was in some way disconcerting. In spite of his strange lethargy he appeared to be in a state of nervous tension, as though, for instance, he was momentarily expecting to be shot from a long way off — as, perhaps, he was! These two states of lethargy and nervous tension sound, I know, impossible to exist at one time, yet they seemed to exist in Eichholz who both bothered and puzzled me. I was continually wanting to ask him what on earth was the matter. His face was lined and warped, it was seared as though by fire, or by some horrible memory; and his eyes, quite round and displaying the entire pupil, moved with reluctant yet continual animation. Yet when he blinked he would sometimes allow his eyes to remain closed for a moment or so, as though dreading the power of vision. I never saw him smile, even the conventional smile which ordinary politeness demands, and I had not observed him for a quarter of an hour before I came to the conclusion that Eichholz was more abjectly miserable than any man I had ever beheld. He seemed horribly, deeply, shockingly unhappy; he appeared sodden with misery, without hope, and though furtively alarmed, only automatically alive. It seemed incredible that a white man should get into such a state, and his state fascinated me against my will. For there was nothing abject about Eichholz, nothing cowardly or contemptible. But it is useless for me to try to describe him; though his astonishingly thin, tall, stooping figure, in rather dirty, ill-cut white clothing, his shaven, twisted face, wide eyes and rather long, untidy grey hair, his prominent ears and pointed nose and chin, and above all his strange atmosphere of utter despair will remain always in my mind. And in the background of my recollection there will always be that mysterious and abysmal forest; in fact, the two seem inseparable, they seem to be cause and effect.

"Mr. Massingbird?" asked Eichholz; "I understood that Mr. Massingbird was coming with you."

For a moment I gazed at his inexplicable face and the power of speech left me. It was the most extraordinary thing I have ever had to say, and with really an immense effort I said it.

"Mr. Massingbird," said I, "went temporarily mad. He drew his revolver on Captain Hawks and I hit him. I hit him with my fist behind the ear and killed him. Mr. Massingbird is dead."

Eichholz rose suddenly from his chair.

CHAPTER VIII

THE BLOWGUN INDIANS

EICHHOLZ walked the length of the bridge, and leaning over the rail addressed the mulatto in command of the river boat in a long, earnest speech in some mongrel Spanish dialect.

I waited a little breathlessly until he returned.

"I was thinking, Mr. Mate," said he, in his easy, idiomatic English, "that it seems a pity to waste time here, and that if my boat cast off, we might proceed to Maloca — eh?"

"Very good," I answered, with smothered astonishment, and rose and issued my orders.

The casting-off of the river steamer was something of a business, and the operation was performed mostly by our men. When this was accomplished, we up-anchored and proceeded, Eichholz's steamer following, and unable to keep pace with us astern. Captain Esterkay took charge, and I conducted Eichholz down to dinner, and he ate with a sudden ravenousness the good food placed before him. It would seem that he had not tasted an appetising meal for a very long time indeed, and it was not until toward the end of dinner that he again referred to Massingbird.

"So Mr. Massingbird died of fever," said he; "well, the fever gets us all in the end."

I stared at him, and he, for a moment, looked me back calmly in the eyes, and his look was the look of a sage regarding a child.

"Mr. Massingbird, as I have told you —" I began.

"I know! I know!" he replied, and held up a long and by no means clean hand with a quiet and subtly superior gesture.

For a moment I was angry; then realising the futility of anger and realising also that I was in a very strange world, indeed, I shut my mouth and grinned. It may not have been a very pleasant grin. For the rest of the meal Eichholz did the talking. He talked, of course, about rubber and the rubber market, the labour difficulties and the river world in general, and he was interesting. Some men can speak of the most trivial matters and attract one's attention at once. Eichholz was one of these, for he had great intelligence, and the more I saw of him the more I wondered how and why such a man came to be banished to this appalling, remote, and savage country. He never asked one question about the world of civilised men that he had left and from which he was so terribly far removed, though it came out casually in conversation that the last time he saw a newspaper was four months before, and it was two months old at the time. But he had heard of Colonel Calvin. That intrepid American had, to use a useful phrase, "painted the Upper Amazon red." Every one knew all about him, or said that they did, and the colonel was in a fair way of becoming a legendary character imbued with almost Jove-like powers. There seemed no doubt at all that the colonel was, indeed, with the Blowgun Indians, and was, moreover, very much alive and kicking. Yet the Blowgun Indians were regarded by the white men and imported negroes with far greater dread than was ever the Apache by the early settlers in the West. And this was not on account of their ferocity, for the Blowgun Indians were not particularly ferocious, — they, in fact, only wished to be let alone, — but it was on account of their horrible weapon and still more horrible ammunition. From Eichholz I got a very complete account of both the Indians and their armament, and I fully confess that I would far sooner be shot at any number of times with a modern rifle than once with a blowgun.

The Indians, by all accounts, were a well-set-up race of people, a light copper in hue and with developed heads and intellects. They moved about very much as they pleased, and though strongly suspected of cannibalism there was, so far, no direct evidence in this direction. The "splendid isolation" afforded them, not only by the nature of the country they inhabited, but more by their shocking weapons, had enabled them to remain practically undisturbed and work out their own destiny along their own lines: though of course any large amount of information concerning them was not to be had, as they made it a sort of matter of principle to shoot all white men on sight. They were able to move about through the most impenetrable forest with easy, soundless speed, and usually the first warning which a man had of having stumbled inadvertently across a Blowgun Indian was a sudden and swift difficulty in breathing. Then a rapidly creeping paralysis caused him first to stumble and then to fall, while he struggled for breath like the drowning. From these symptoms he might know that he had been shot by a Blowgun Indian and that his inevitable death would take place not more than four minutes later. Such a death, I take it, was enough to scare any man; it was certainly enough to scare me!

The blowgun is from six to eight feet long, with a most ingenious mouthpiece at the heavy end. The darts used, and which the Indians

can blow with complete accuracy up to thirty
yards (a longer range was unnecessary, anyway, in such a country), were supposed to be
about five inches long, but Eichholz thought
that they were considerably shorter. These
darts, as sharply pointed as it was possible to
get them and hardly of a greater diameter than
a steel knitting-needle, revolve rapidly in flight
by means of a spiral twist of raw cotton, as an
arrow revolves in flight by means of the feathers
in its shaft. The discharge and passage of the
dart are, of course, soundless, and a man surrounded by stinging insects, scratched and raked
by thorny branches, and tangled up in a mass of
resisting vegetation would, as like as not, never
notice the minute, needle-like puncture of the
dart through a thin cotton shirt, or in bare neck,
arms, or shoulders. And to puncture the skin is
all that is necessary. Once the blood is reached,
nothing on earth can save him, and he is doomed
to death by the most horrible form of suffoca-
tion. For the *curare* with which the darts are
tipped does not, strangely enough, affect the
heart. The paralysis it causes only prevents a
man from inflating and deflating the lungs, a
fate shocking enough to contemplate; yet, Colonel Ezra Calvin, that amazing New Englander,
was apparently living amicably in the midst of the
Blowgun Indians and their wonderful weapons.

As that day passed and we continued up-stream, there was abundant evidence of the changing nature of the country. The current of the river grew swifter and the banks higher, rising even at times to low cliffs of clay, with here and there an outcrop of stones. But there was plenty of room for the *Martin Connor*, at any rate, at that time of year, and toward sunset we opened out a clearing that marked the up-country headquarters of the Rio Maloca Rubber Company, one of the tentacles, as it were, of the octopus-like Rio Maranon Rubber Company.

The clearing was, perhaps, some ten or twelve acres in extent, the forest surrounding it on three sides. As the ultimate end of a considerable voyage it seemed inadequate and hardly worth a place on the map. The house of Eichholz, a six-roomed dwelling on stilts, stood apart, with a flagstaff bearing the tattered remains of a flag before it. Behind this there stood a number of long buildings used as storehouses, while a square thatched roof upon eight or ten tree-trunk pillars gave shelter to the first process which the newly gathered rubber underwent, where, in fact, it was changed from the cream-like substance produced by the trees to lumps of soft consistency, worth about a dollar a kilogramme in Maloca and worth twice as much in

Para. The time that we were there was the time of a rubber boom, and the rubber companies and company promoters were rolling in money. For an establishment of a rich combine, Maloca was surprising; it suggested the results of costly litigation and a fallen market. But we were new to the Amazonian way of doing business, which way is, perhaps, the most stupid and extraordinary in the world. For years the people of the Amazon Valley have sacrificed everything, including the river Indians, to the collection of rubber. They have planted nothing, not even rubber trees to any extent, and they have wholly neglected all cultivation of foodstuffs. Not only have they no manufactures, but the customs tariffs are of such a character that it is impossible for them to manufacture anything in the country with a profit. Everything, be it the most trivial and everyday necessities like butter or eggs or cheese, must be imported in sealed tins and pay an enormous import duty, and life in an Amazonian swamp is about as expensive as life on Fifth Avenue or in Park Lane. Surrounded by a profligacy of nature that amazes the eye, Eichholz was living on canned meat from Chicago, tinned butter and awfully preserved eggs from Denmark, eating off English plates on English tables and drinking Scotch whiskey, and doing so at a really stupendous cost — this upon a waterway, long, it is true, yet leading to all the ends of the earth without necessary transhipment. I was inclined to agree with Wilfred, whose economical domestic policy was shocked at these conditions.

"These 'ere people," remarked the little man, who had been making pointed enquiries, "are mad or drunk. This country is fair rottin' wiv money, or the prospec's of money, an' all they do is to collec' their bloomin' old rubber and collec' it in sech a manner as ter kill the trees. W'at's the sense of it, fer the goodness sake? Hey?"

"Climate," said I.

And Cert'nly Wilfred intimated his doubts of the accuracy of my statement.

"Yer a liar," said he, "it ain't. Hit's natural-born wickedness, which is only another name fer a particular kind of stupidity. Hi jes' don't hunderstand it, no Hi don't. Hi ain't no commercial man, though maybe Hi 'ave got a tidy little sum put by in the London General. But even *Hi* can see what could be done 'ere."

"Theoretically —" I began.

"Ain't got no use fer theories. Theories is one of the things what people invent instead of workin'. What's wanted 'ere is a practical happlication of ordinary common sense along business lines. Like what a frien' of mine in London did and does. 'E's in the 'at-guard line."

"Hat-guard?" I asked wonderingly.

"Yus, 'at-guard. You know, 'e sells strings what yer farsten to yer 'at to keep it from blowin' away. Got the point? Well, they costs 'im, my frien', these 'at-guards do, tuppince a dozen all farstened ready to a card with a pitcher of the King on it wearin' one. Now, my frien', 'e don't sell 'em at tuppince each on Ludgit 'Ill as most others do. 'E's got henterprise an' 'e sells 'is bloomin' 'at-guards at sixpince heach on the 'scursion boats sailin' from London Bridge for Soufend, Clacton, and Ramsgit. 'E goes aboard an' swears blind it's goin' ter blow, puts on a jersey an' makes out 'e's a sailor, though 'e's bin on nothink more than the Serpintine. Well, it gen'rally does blow in England, we ain't smooth-water people, and any man that ain't a mug would sooner pay sixpince fer an 'at-guard than lose a three an' ninepenny Dunn. Theoretically, my frien' is makin' an outrageous profit, but 'e ain't reely. 'Cause why? 'Cause 'e 'as a right to 'is sixpince, not because 'e jest can get it, not because 'e arsks fer it, but because 'e's got the bloomin' sense to take 'is 'at-guards wheer they are worth sixpince of anybody's money. That's efficiency, that is, an' no bloomin' theories — see?"

"But I don't see how that applies —" I began.

"'Ere!" broke in Wilfred; "I've got seven joints of meat roasting in the galley an' you keep me talkin' 'alf the day — you the mate of this ship! You should know better, George 'En-ery Grummet!" — and he hurried off to the galley.

The coming alongside the wharf at Maloca was a delicate business, for the wharf was as fragile as a frame house. As the captain was too ill with fever, the job fell to me, and I had all that I could do not to root the crazy structure from its foundations. It was built for river boats and not ocean-going steamers, and I had profound misgivings whether it could hold us when we were there. So I sent out a kedge and warped in, holding to the river bed more than to the wharf, and by nightfall we were tied up, officially at our journey's end.

It was now, and for the first time, that we came in actual and regular contact with the shore, and there was much of astonishing interest to a man with eyes in his head. The rubber grew wild in the forest and was gathered in a liquid state by the Indians, who, cutting the tree-trunk in a certain manner, tapped and collected the milky juice known as "latex." This latex of the best trees and plants furnished from twenty to fifty per cent of rubber, and what precisely this juice is, or what part it plays in the organism of the tree, nobody seemed to know, for it was not the sap of the tree, being found just under the bark and outside the wood proper. Though it appeared like milk it did not taste the same, for Wilfred tried it. Yet its resemblance to milk is remarkable, for when left to stand it produced "cream." This cream was called "caoutchouc," if I remember right, pronounced like a sneeze. This stuff gradually coagulated and became solid, the process being facilitated by the introduction of certain chemicals that vary according to the latex gathered. When the latex began to solidify, it was rolled into a more or less spherical shape, and was added to by pouring fresh latex over it until the mass arrived at a convenient weight and size for handling. It was odd thus to see rubber poured from a tin jug; and, as Wilfred said, it seemed a long way off a taxicab! At the time that we were there the settlement was almost empty, as large quantities of rubber had come in recently and the Indians had been forced to go farther afield. Why precisely the Indians consented to gather rubber we were at a loss to discover. Their payment was a farce, and they were, practically speaking, slaves, and atrociously treated slaves at that. There was a gang of negro overseers that gave both Captain Hawks and myself some uneasiness. Clad in tattered canvas trousers and wide-brimmed hats, they strolled about armed with modern rifles, and their manners, to put it delicately, were not what they should have been. Their constitutions were better fitted to stand the climate than those of the alleged white men, who, fever-racked, lonely, and debased, did not show up to advantage. Moreover, it was the duty of these negroes to drive the Indians, and they drove them without mercy, pity, or compassion. The bearing, therefore, of these overseers was next thing to impossible, and a conflict with our crew seemed inevitable. Once the trouble began, unless we could stop it, Maloca and its negro and possibly white population would get wiped off the map.

Three days after we had arrived, and while we were busy discharging cargo, a large buck negro, clad in the usual ragged trousers and hat and with the inevitable machete at his belt, came lounging aboard as though he owned the ship and discovered Wilfred at work in the galley. The negro spoke English (he, like the rest, came from Barbadoes), and leaning easily at the galley door, he observed the little cook breaking up a large piece of coal in order to get it into the stove. Wilfred was busy and did not see the negro at first, and Wilfred, clad in a shirt and cotton trousers, looked very small, indeed. So the negro laughed and remarked upon Wilfred's stature, and Wilfred, never slow at repartee, turned about and replied with the iron hammer in his hand at the moment, and the negro went to sleep for a long time. This caused irritation, and matters were not made better by a second negro, engaged to assist us to land cargo, spitting on the forward main-deck. Now, there was an unwritten law in the *Martin Connor* that, though you could spit if you wanted to, you might not spit except overside. An altercation followed, the negro was insolent, and Timothy Hanks, who was in charge, hit him all over the forward deck until he was carried ashore by his friends. The following day a third negro arrived, one chosen by his fellows, and demanded to see Captain Hawks. He was interviewed by myself. He demanded reparation on behalf of his two friends, who appeared to be the worse for wear. I answered that I thought no reparation was necessary as, in the first place, a negro had made an uncalled-for personal remark to a white man, and in the second, a negro had infringed a by-law of the ship and had been insolent when rebuked. The negro who had come to see Captain Hawks then became abusive, and he was landed later by means of one of the forward derricks at the moment engaged in hoisting carboys of chemicals from the hold. That began the trouble with the negro overseers, who, with firearms, and machetes, and with no adequate authority over them, were a distinct source of danger. As our men were itching to "man-handle" every darky in the place, Captain Hawks, Timothy Hanks, myself, and the engineers had all we could do to prevent really serious consequences.

But to keep the men aboard when work was over not only was impossible, but would have been unjust. They had every right to go ashore, and ashore they went, but always in numbers, and they brought back some astonishing things to the ship. Whenever they chanced across Indians who knew them to be off the *Martin Connor*, whose favourable reputation had preceded her by means of Indian "wireless," a good deal of trading took place, which trading was strictly prohibited by the Rio Maloca Rubber Company. But for my part I could not see why our men should not trade if they wished. By what right a certain body of men can assume ownership over a vast tract of country which they fail to civilise, survey, or even explore, I do not know, neither did our men. I put the situation to the captain, who answered: "Let 'em go ahead, Grummet; I'm sick to death of these rubber trusts anyway." So the men went ahead, and for the first time in their lives the Indians had a chance of fair and just bargains, whereby

every man in the forecastle and Wilfred in the
galley accumulated rubber that was worth considerably more than their wages for the entire
trip; rubber which, however, was eventually
thrown overside.

The difficulties that arose over landing the
cargo at Maloca caused my commander to
make one of his rare speeches to the crew. He
explained that there was, apparently, no one at
Maloca to unload the ship. He admitted that
there were the negroes, but the negroes were
employed by Eichholz for the Rio Maloca Rubber Company, and were not his — Captain
Hawks's — to order about. Although he knew
that the crew had signed on to work the ship
and not her cargo, her cargo would rot in the
hold unless the crew unloaded her. Therefore
he would be obliged to them if they would consider the situation and decide to meet him in the
difficulty of their own accord; since, if they did
not, he would be under the unpleasant necessity
of making them. Each man should earn full
stevedore's wages for the period plus their ordinary pay, and any negro that happened to be
knocking about and who the crew thought
might be useful in the hold — why — he left it
to them to decide what was the best thing to
do. But there must be no actual trouble, or he
would see to it personally — he would come down

to the main-deck or into the forecastle if necessary — he would see to it personally that the
crew had as unpleasant a time as any man
"there among you" has had inside or outside
jail.

The crew stood and grinned; they were a joy
to behold. They all wore hats, for hats were a
necessity, but otherwise their clothing was not
of a ceremonious nature, though 'Arry Ketchold
wore a shirt as well as trousers in honour of the
dignity of his position as boatswain. They were
hairy and muscular, they were truculent and
cheerful, and they grinned at the captain with
real, genuine affection. This was man-talk and
they understood it. They also understood that
Captain Hawks could, there and then, did he
choose, thrash any three of them simultaneously
with his bare fists, let alone what he could do
with a belaying pin and a gun. He was the best
man in the ship; they were prepared to go ashore
and tell Maloca that Captain Hawks was the
best man in South America, in North America,
in the Western Hemisphere — in the whole
world; and they intimated their willingness to
work cargo through the boatswain, who, thus
cast into sudden prominence, was stricken with
stage fright, and in consequence discovered his
voice in the top of his head. This caused a man
behind him to let out a laugh, whereby he re-

ceived a back-handed blow from 'Arry Ketchold, delivered surreptitiously, that would have felled an ox.

The next negro that strolled aboard vanished. He was promptly and silently confiscated and set to work in the hold, and we had no more bother with them. Thus the cargo that came aboard at Galveston was whipped out in record time, and the cargo that was awaiting us in the storehouses was brought down to the wharf by Indians, ready to be put aboard.

Meanwhile our bill-of-fare was undergoing some startling changes due to enterprising experiments by Wilfred with the local productions. Timothy Hanks was our sportsman assisted by one of the crew, and the bag often contained a variety that ranged from wild ducks in abundance, turkeys, doves, and unknown birds to a young tapir or two. This last, the tapir, is a wild (very, very wild) hog, and when young is excellent eating. Wilfred experimented in smoking tapir meat, and built himself a smokehouse on the after main-deck, and after nearly suffocating us all he got his machinery in order and produced what was every bit as good as the best Yorkshire hams, and Yorkshire, England, beats any place I have ever been to, so far as pork is considered. Then Wilfred tried smoking manatee meat, but this was not a success, so he tried pickling and nearly pickled himself, for he fell into the vat. His pickling was an advanced sort of pickling, almost scientific, needing changes of flavouring at extraordinary hours of the night and morning, and after a lengthy and complicated process his production was not unlike inferior beef with a strong medicinal flavour. So he gave up experimenting in that direction and the manatees went to Percy, the alligator, who was now, if not tame, not quite so violently disposed to man. But your real artist cannot always be successful; a man who cannot make mistakes cannot make anything, and Wilfred's pickling and smoking operations were a source of great interest to us all, for with these strange and unknown animals one never knew what he would produce. He never knew himself, for though the Indians and the white men had eaten most of these animals and birds with which he experimented, their efforts had been crude and devoid of that touch of genius which Wilfred possessed and by which we all benefited.

With the tapirs, however, he was uniformly successful and happy in his results, and, incidentally, so were we. As, at length, he carried his operations to such an extent as materially to reduce the expenditure of ship's stores, Captain Hawks arranged with Timothy Hanks (an inveterate sportsman) that he should spend more time with his gun, and should have two men regularly to help him. The tapirs swarmed in uncounted multitudes and averaged a good three foot to the shoulder. They were as much at home in the water as on land, and they would gladly fight anything. When startled they would career through the underbrush, their leathern hides remaining unhurt by the worst thorns, and as they generally came for you like a large projectile, the hunting of the tapirs was not without incident, for the tapir always meant business. They were a light brown in colour, had fighting eyes, and made sounds like other pigs, though the sounds were more warlike than is the voice of our homely porker. When we arrived home, long after, I looked up "tapir" in a well-known and highly respected encyclopædia and read: "The tapir can be brought under the subjection of man and is easily tamed." This was not our experience, which leads me to conclude that there must be a mistake somewhere, for the tapirs which we encountered would most certainly not come under the subjection of man until they were very dead, indeed; and would have charged a battleship in the water, or a fifty-storied steel-construction building on land. No, there were "no flies" on the tapirs; we liked them, for they seemed to be the only thoroughly sane and healthy creatures in the Amazon Valley except, maybe, the Blowgun Indians.

Then there was the manatee. As I had not heard of this beast before I was up the Amazon, perhaps I might be permitted to explain that the manatee is one of the family rejoicing in the generic name of *Sirenia*, and that the manatee looks Teutonic in origin. It is, however, not Teutonic in character. Ten or twelve feet in length seemed to be the average size of the manatee, and all the specimens which we saw seemed to be affected with profound lethargy. It lives in the water, and is in striking contrast with the rest of the violent and intense life of the Amazon jungle. All the other creatures resent man's intrusion in unmistakeable terms, but the manatee just sleeps when he is alive, and is just dead when he is dead. A slumberous disregard of danger that is half pathetic and half unreasonably stupid has saved the manatee from the fate of the more warlike and active. And so the manatee lives on, not often awake, never quite sure that he is alive; and that is about all there is to say of the manatee. I have met some people like manatees.

As for the birds, the pigeons, the turkeys, the doves, and the many others which we could not name, we had them in stews, in pies, on

toast, and in casseroles. We lived like kings
and princes with a great variety of menu, which
no doubt had an excellent effect upon us, for
I am convinced that bad and monotonous food
plays no small part in the great Amazon tragedy.
In such a climate the most healthy appetite
fails and must be tempted by succulent fare, as
we found to be the case when Wilfred's turn
came to go down with fever. You just did not
want to eat, so you gradually ate less and less;
this was so with all of us; but when Wilfred
recovered and was up and about again, our
appetites miraculously returned.

And then there came a rude interruption to
our pleasant active life. A stern wheeler arrived from down-stream flying the flag of the
mighty Rio Maranon Rubber Company, and
she was full and bulging with men.

We had, by then, been a week or ten days at
Maloca, and had discharged our cargo and were
an empty ship, a fact that played no small part
in the events to come. The stern wheeler
dropped anchor smartly enough in midstream,
and she showed in her management and general
condition a marked difference from the average
river craft and especially from Eichholz's steamer
that was moored to the river bank to give us
room at the wharf.

A flat-bottomed boat put off from the Rio

Maranon steamer and came punting across toward us. Besides the men propelling the boat, there were two men with rifles and a stout individual with an official bearing.

" 'Ello!" remarked Wilfred, who was smoking a cigarette near the gangplank, " 'ere 's Uncle Boffin from Palmer's Green!"

The boat came round our bows and up to the wharf, and the stout man and the two men carrying rifles climbed the short bamboo ladder, gained the wharf, then marched aboard us without invitation.

" 'Ere!" expostulated Wilfred smartly, "this 'ere's private property, old dear!"

The stout man, who was followed closely by the two men with the rifles, paid not the very least attention to Wilfred's existence.

"Now, see 'ere, Willy," remarked the little cook, "none o' thet, if you please, or you'll get sech a masher in yer eye thet you'll wish you'd never, never seen me!" And Wilfred promptly laid a restraining though perfectly civil hand on the stout man's arm, for the stout man was briskly aiming for the port alleyway, as though intent upon gaining the main cabin. The effect of this action was instantaneous. The stout man rapped out an order, and the two men with rifles sent Wilfred skittling across the deck as though he had been a child. Up till then I had been watching, but at that I interfered, and I did so without loss of time, for I was more than a little angry. But quick though I may have been I did not arrive before the little cook had planted a very sharp and nasty blow under the chin of one of the men with rifles. He had aimed for the man's eye, but could n't reach, and my arrival was just in time to prevent the other man from felling the cook with the butt of his rifle. I hit that man, I hit him as hard as I could, and meanwhile the stout man clapped a whistle to his mouth and blew an echoing screech and started running for the main cabin. I turned after him and grabbed him by his white coat collar, and to my considerable astonishment he unhesitatingly drew a revolver. By this time you can imagine that I was really angry, more with the impudence of the proceeding than with anything else.

"You idiot!" I cried angrily and wrenched the pistol from his hand. The weapon went off with a bang, a bang that summoned every one to the spot.

"What" — enquired the captain arriving in a hurry, — "what's this?"

"I don't know what it is, sir," I replied, holding my man tightly, "but it marched aboard and tried to shoot me."

The stout man instantly burst into the most

rapid speech I have ever heard; it was like the rattling of a machine, speech which none of us except Captain Esterkay could understand; and glancing over my shoulder toward the newly arrived Rio Maranon steamer I noticed that two boats full of men were putting off and aiming for the shore.

Captain Esterkay whistled in astonishment.

"He's come to arrest Grummet!" cried the Southerner in sudden alarm; "he's come to arrest Grummet for killing that bug Massingbird! Say, Matthew, here's trouble!"

And then several things happened at once.

CHAPTER IX

To begin with, our crew, deckhands and stokers alike, raised up their voices and, in different tones but with a common note of exultation, cried: "Hooray! He's come to arrest the mate! Let's go and wreck their mud-pusher!!"

Captain Hawks gave one glance at the two boatfuls of armed men hurrying toward the wharf, and grasping my prisoner by the slack of his pants and the collar of his coat he ran him with great speed into the lamp locker. During his sudden, violent, and most undignified progress, the stout man's anger caused him to make noises like the squealing of a pig, to the uproarious merriment of the crew, who refused to be silenced by a loud order from myself. There was certainly a humorous side to the affair, but they should not have laughed at an adversary who was getting the worst of it. Into the oily locker went that stout, self-important official; he went with an impetus and rapidity that must have startled him, and I have seldom seen a man handled so completely. It was like a

HE RAN HIM WITH GREAT SPEED INTO THE LAMP LOCKER

conjuring trick, — one moment the man was in our midst, the next and he was in the lamp locker, the iron door, which fastened outside, slammed and bolted.

"For land's sake, Matthew!" gasped Captain Esterkay, while angry bangs and screeches came from within the locker, interspersed with the splintering tinkle of broken glass which told eloquently of the prisoner's state of mind; "for land's sake, Matthew, that man is a commandant —"

"I don't care who or what he is!" said the captain savagely. "He tried to shoot my mate!" And then to the men — "Draw in that gangplank!"

The crew, in a body, rushed to obey, just as the armed men from the two boats began to arrive upon the wharf.

"Now get under cover," was the next order, and the men dropped behind the iron bulwarks grinning broadly.

The ship was some three feet out from the wharf, and owing to our empty holds some eight or ten feet above it. To board her without gangplank or ladder was impossible, and over the bulwarks leaned Captain Hawks with a large revolver in his hand. The men from the boats arrived one by one and paused upon the wharf uncertain what to do, though some of them fingered their rifles with practised and itching fingers. They were a hard-looking set, and though ragged they had all the appearance of ruthless self-assurance that marks the desperado. Meanwhile, the two attendants who had come aboard with our prisoner were being silently and most efficiently bound up by our crouching crew.

"Ask them," said Captain Hawks to Captain Esterkay, "what they want, who they are, and by what right they board my ship?"

Captain Esterkay turned to the wharf. Meanwhile the yells and thumps from within the locker continued. Captain Esterkay finished speaking and a man on the wharf made reply. He was apparently second in command, and he seemed both surprised and angry.

"He says," interpreted Captain Esterkay, who was now as bland and as unruffled as ever, — "he says that it is on a charge of murdering Massingbird that they wish to arrest Grummet; that they represent the Rio Maranon Rubber Company, which company holds itself responsible for the law and order — the *law and order*, Matthew — of this forgotten country; and I gather that the gentleman inside the locker is some one of considerable importance, though I did n't catch his name. They say that unless we let out their commander, and that quick too, they will come aboard and arrest the ship."

"Ask 'em," said Captain Hawks, "to come right aboard and do so — if they can."

"You mean it, Matthew?" enquired Captain Esterkay calmly; "just remember who you are dealing with."

"Go ahead, Alexander."

And Captain Esterkay turned to the men on the wharf.

"All the men aboard?" asked the captain while Captain Esterkay was speaking, and as it happened to be the dinner hour they were.

"Yes, sir," I answered, "all hands aboard."

"Steam?" asked Captain Hawks, and Mr. McLushley, who stood smiling sardonically in the background, answered softly: "Drawn fires. Steam in an hour's time, not less," and vanished, taking his three engineers with him and the stoke-hold watch.

The effect of what Captain Esterkay said was visible. The men on the wharf started promptly looking for some method of boarding the ship. There was nothing backward about those men.

"Ask them," said Captain Hawks, "whether they would like their commander now, or if they would like to wait until they get him."

"Hush, Matthew, don't yo' make bad worse. The shootin' 'll start quick enough."

"Cast off those shore lines," said the captain to me; "you will have to cut them. If any one on the wharf draws a bead on you while you are doing so I'll drop him in his tracks."

I jumped at his bidding and with me jumped the happy crew, who were deeply pleased with everything, especially the prospect of a quite uncommon scrap. And meanwhile the gentleman in the lamp locker had almost, but not quite, screeched himself voiceless.

I have already explained that, fearing the wharf was not adequate to hold the ship, I had sent out a kedge to prevent us from pressing too hard against the wharf. This kedge, therefore, was some distance out in the river. The moment that the shore lines were parted the winch was set going, and the ship glided out and put a good ten yards between herself and the wharf when we let go the port anchor. We were now, practically speaking, impregnable to anything short of artillery, for we were like a castle surrounded by a moat, and the moat in our case swamped with alligators and a particular kind of fish that was more ferocious than a rattlesnake.

"I guess we can come to terms," said the captain with a grin, and threw open the door of the lamp locker.

The man inside was now silent. A colossal pride of office, a soured, acid, and peevish temper had been violently outraged in a tropical climate, and the man looked shattered, as though by an illness.

"Snakes!" exclaimed the captain, with surprise; "say, Alexander, ask him to step out and come to the cabin where we can talk this matter over."

And a moment later the three men disappeared from view.

"Better unlash those two men," said I; and the two disarmed men were set free.

Meanwhile the men upon the wharf had gathered into a bunch and were evidently holding a council of war. I watched them carefully. For though it was not likely that they would fire upon us while their commander and two of their number were still our prisoners, they might; and I sent Wilfred for his revolver, for Wilfred was next thing to a miracle with a gun.

"If any man there shoots at us," said I, "let him have it."

"I will!" answered the cook with great gusto, proceeding to load his forty-four Smith and Wesson in a manner that bordered upon sleight of hand.

The little man then sat himself upon a bollard and watched the wharf intently, longingly, and — cheerfully, whistling softly —

> "We don't want to lose you,
> But we think you ought to go!"

There then passed a period of waiting, the engineers and the stokers alone being busy. The men on the wharf were joined by the thin, stooping figure of Eichholz, who waved his hand to me with an impartial gesture, as though he wished to demonstrate that he, personally, had nothing to do with this trouble, and I waved back friendlily to him. I had a liking for Eichholz, he was so intelligent, and he was a picturesque figure in a drab world of mediocre villains. The time dragged on, and Eichholz got himself into a dugout and letting down the ladder, I awaited his coming. He climbed aboard and shook hands with me.

"This is bad," said he, gazing vaguely about the ship and hardly looking at me; "I'm afraid that you are in for real serious trouble. You are a very long way from Para," he added. And then, after a pause, he continued, "I have just received orders per the Maranon boat not to supply you with your return cargo. This, in itself, means a heavy financial loss — to return with an empty ship."

"But are agreements not worth the paper they are written on?" I asked. "The return cargo was guaranteed."

"Nothing's guaranteed here. Nothing — life — property — or" — and his face twisted suddenly — "honour."

It was on the end of my tongue to exclaim, "Skittles!" but I refrained, for the man's manner was impressive, and quite suddenly I had an inspiration. "Why," I asked, "do you stay here, Eichholz?" And to my simple question he turned upon me a startled gaze.

"Why?" he asked, as though my question had been most extraordinary, "why? Because I can't get away, of course!"

"Can't get away?" I repeated; "what d'you mean?"

"Can't get away; can't do it. They have got me tight!" he said. And just then Captain Hawks came striding out of the cabin onto the main-deck followed by our erstwhile prisoner. They stood for a moment by the bulwarks while the stout man hailed his men upon the wharf. The men answered, and then, rather reluctantly, they re-embarked in their boats and started back to their river steamer. Captain Hawks crossed the deck and shook hands with Eichholz and invited him into the cabin, and with a nod to me Eichholz followed the captain and the stout representative of the Rio Maranon Company.

"This 'ere," remarked Wilfred, now relieved from his position on guard by the departure of the men from the wharf, "is jes' a bloomin' frorst, thet's what it is! I thought there was goin' ter be a reel how-d'-y'-do an' instead it's turned out a sort of Hague Peace Conference. Lot o' silly rot, I calls it. Presumably, Mr. Mate, I can retire, since them flat-'eads is gone?"

"You can," said I, grinning at the little man's huge disgust.

"All I can say," he remarked over his thin shoulder, as he strolled off, "is, that if any bloke shut me up in a lamp locker there'd be trouble fer some one when I got out. I wouldn't take it sweet an' kind like our friend Willy in the cabin. An' as fer 'is crowd thet was on the wharf, if I'd been them I wouldn't 'ave jes' stood theer and spat in the water, no, I wouldn't!" And the little cook went off with a disgusted and contemptuous glance at the two boatloads of men that were now nearing their ship.

"Ain't there goin' to be no scrap, sir?" breathed a man deferentially in my ear. "Can't we go across an' wreck their mud-pusher?"

"No, you can't," I answered, in no uncertain tone; "you'll stay aboard, every mother's son of you."

What was going on in the cabin I did not know, but there seemed to be a deadlock, and there then fell one of those trying times of idleness when anything can happen and when there is nothing to do. As night came on I wandered

about the ship restlessly watching the settlement twinkle into being, and the river boat il-
lumine herself garishly with oil lamps that cast
out long, streaming reflections, and then, quite
suddenly, the conference in the cabin apparently grew acute. Loud voices raised in anger
came from the four men within as though they
had all lost their tempers together, and Wilfred,
in his galley, laughed.

"Like a bloomin' monkey house!" he commented.

Then the voices fell again and we continued
our restless waiting. Some Indians put out
from the bank in dugouts and canoes to fish, as
they did every evening; I counted six, and having nothing else to do I leaned upon the rail and
idly watched them in the gathering gloom sliding noiselessly over the lead-coloured surface
of the river. And then, imperceptibly, the six
canoes became seven, and where or how they
were joined by the seventh I could not tell. I
counted them afresh, for it was something to do,
and discovered that there were eight. I puzzled
in a half-interested fashion over this incident,
and counting them again I found that there were
ten. I became interested then. You must remember that the light was almost gone, but that
the surface of the river reflected the sky, and
was still a luminous expanse, fading toward the

other bank, and each canoe floated upon its perfect reflection. Moreover, when they chanced to come together, it was not easy to distinguish them, and they became one dark mass. Yet this mysterious process of addition went on; and at last, thoroughly puzzled, I called Timothy Hanks.

"How many canoes do you see there?" I asked him, and he counted them with difficulty owing to the rapidly failing light.

"Eighteen, I make it," said he.

"Now, d' you mind counting them again?" I asked, and he did so.

"Say!" he exclaimed, "what's the matter with me! There's twenty-five now! Some must have come down a creek to one side, but I did n't see 'em arrive!"

"And now there's thirty-three," said I.

"No, forty! My! My! Those canoes seem to come just the way the Apaches were said to show up in the old days in the West! One minute there was an empty landscape, and the next the place was full of 'em. Now, ain't that just remarkable?"

The river steamer was lit like a theatre and was a spot of brilliance in the deepening night. There came from her the multitudinous Babel of many voices, and through an open doorway upon her upper deck we could see four men seated at cards. The canoes drifted down-stream, silent and ghostlike, some passing on the far side of the river steamer, others drifting down between the two vessels, and from among these last one canoe detached itself and came with sudden swiftness toward us. I cannot tell what was the precise difference between that canoe and the many others which we had seen at intervals on our journey up-stream, but a difference there was, a difference that at once caught my attention and held it. As an artist will regard a foreign painting with understanding discrimination, so will the sailor observe the handling and character of a strange craft. That canoe was longer, more narrow than those we had seen the river Indians using, and the manner in which that canoe was handled was something of a revelation. And at the approach of that canoe, Maryjane, our one-legged patient, now hopping about with the aid of a crutch (he could not as yet bear his stump upon a peg), showed sudden signs of great excitement not unmixed with fear. It was then that I began to have an inkling of who and what those Indians were, and I confess to an unpleasant catch of the breath. The canoe came sweeping along-side with an elegant ease that was good to behold, and leaning out over the bulwarks I stared down into her and beheld three naked men at the paddles, while a fourth, a fine, slim specimen, stood up in an attitude full of grace, holding aloft at arm's length a stick. In a cleft in the end of the stick was a piece of folded paper. He thrust it at me without a word, and to take the paper thus offered was a natural impulse.

"Who are you from?" I asked, but without answer of any kind the canoe shot off silently, like a fish, into the night.

I took the paper into the light of the alleyway and found it to be a page torn out of a pocket diary, for at the top was a printed date some two years old. The paper was folded, and as the sender seemingly had no envelope the address was written on the paper itself and the message was directed to "The Master of the American ship now at Maloca." That was all.

I felt that this was a matter of importance, and so I put my head into the main cabin, the door of which was open like all doors in the ship for better ventilation, and I found therein some kind of crisis. The occupants had risen to their feet, and I discovered them in various attitudes about the table. The captain leaned upon his arms, his hands spread out upon the table, frowning across at our erstwhile prisoner, who, with folded arms and head thrown back, exhibited (I could not help but think it, considering his circumstances) a rather gallant defiance. Captain Esterkay, with a worried, pained expression upon his usually urbane features, was absently searching himself for a cigar; while Eichholz, his high, narrow forehead corrugated with parallel lines, gazed sorrowfully at the middle of the table. It was ridiculously like a scene from some rather cheap melodrama, yet its intensity was obvious and I positively feared the interruption I should cause, for it was plain to the dullest that death lurked just round the corner, and any interruption might hasten its coming. Then the captain caught sight of me in the doorway and the spell was broken.

"What is it?" he asked, and the four men about the table moved, came out of their attitudes as it were, as people do after standing to be photographed.

"Can I have a word with you, sir?" I asked, and the captain nodded and joined me in the alleyway. I gave him the note, and he read the inscription half aloud, and then unfolding the message he glanced at the bottom for the signature of the sender. As he did so he slapped his thigh with a crack like a pistol and twisted the paper round for me to see.

I read: "*Yours faithfully, Ezra Calvin.*"

"When and how did this come?" asked Captain Hawks, and while I told him he swept his eyes through the letter, then returned to the beginning and read it slowly, thoughtfully, with wide eyes of acute interest. Having finished reading it a second time he looked at me with tremendous animation in his expression, an animation that was so exultant that I felt that had he not been a man possessing great self-control he would have shouted. Then he read the note a third time with slow deliberation. Then, putting it away in his pocket with care, he stood a moment in thought.

"Have all ready to up anchor in ten minutes' time," said he, suddenly, briskly, and turned back to the cabin. As I hurried off I heard his voice raised loudly, ringingly, as though offering an ultimatum.

The night was now fully arrived, and with it had come a high fog that obscured the stars and it was very dark. Considering the narrowness of the river, to move at all from anchor was a form of lunacy difficult to name, but orders are orders, and I at once sent word of warning to Mr. McLushley. I spoke to the chief myself through the charthouse tube.

"Intends to get under weigh now?" enquired the Scotchman, — and I could hear his astonished voice echoing in his silent engine-room, — "man, he's daft!"

I then hauled short on the cable, and the noise of the steam capstan seemed terrific in that still night and brought about a sudden activity on board the river boat which promptly hailed us in some form of Spanish. They thought, perhaps, that we were going to run off with their valuable commander.

"Speak English!" I shouted back, but after once hailing they were silent.

Captain Hawks, followed by the others, came out of the cabin, and the representative of the Rio Maranon Rubber Company hailed his river steamer, which at once put off a boat with all the clatter and fuss of the landsman when dealing with the water, be it in rowing boats or yachts. The stout man then went down the ladder I lowered for him, followed by the two men who had accompanied him aboard. He said never a word, and he carried off this ignominious proceeding with his head up, whereat we all thought the better of him. We had, apparently, refused to be arrested!

Then Eichholz said farewell, and I recollect that I was sorry to see him go, for I was still longing to know just why he could not leave Maloca and in what way the Rio Maranon held him so tight. And the moment he had gone every light went out in the ship, with the exception of those in the engine-room, one of the engineers himself covering the skylights with a tarpaulin. They must have suffered considerably from the heat so caused, but they made no complaints. For every one in the ship was aware of the captain's intention of getting under weigh, and what I might describe as a strain of exhilarating madness went through every man aboard, giving each a stealthy energy. Those were fine moments!

"Let that kedge go," came the captain's quiet voice from the invisible bridge, "and up with your anchor, Grummet."

"Aye, aye, sir!" I answered, and the roaring of the capstan drowned all other sounds for some moments.

"All clear, sir!" I called.

It was an odd experience and will remain vividly in my mind, the experience of getting an unlit steamer from her anchorage and proceeding up an unlit river a thousand miles from the sea in a darkness that you could positively feel. The wildest excitement prevailed upon the river boat, and for a moment they were of a mind to follow us. But they gave up the attempt, and contented themselves with shooting at where they judged us to be from the sound of the engines and the noise that the slow-moving propeller made in the water. The bullets sang merrily about us, or hit the ship with loud, ringing reports when they hit iron or with sharp thuds if they encountered rare wood. But they had jumped to the conclusion that we intended going down-stream, and so we moved, in time, out of the area of their fire, though it was not until some minutes had passed, and during those minutes it was not altogether pleasant.

Standing right in the bows I stared ahead, but stare as I would I could make nothing of the darkness. I knew by the feel of the ship that the captain was groping his way as a man gropes with outstretched arms in a dark room. Not a voice was raised above a whisper, that all orders from the bridge might be instantly heard, and the men, cheerfully subdued, went about with bare feet, active, eager, and happy. There was only the throb of the engines going dead slow.

One by one the scattered lights of Maloca disappeared, obscured suddenly by intervening masses of foliage. It was a period of suspense, and my eyes, strained and staring, peopled the night with phantoms.

"Can you see anything at all, Grummet?" came Captain Hawks's voice from the bridge, raised just enough to carry, and with a calm, unhurried utterance.

"Nothing much, sir, I answered, — "twenty yards at most."

The lights of the settlement had now vanished; the night closed in upon us with palpable intensity, and an instinctive habit long acquired afforded me a mental chart of our progress.

The engine-room bell clattered loudly, and the vibration of the engines ceased, followed by a great aching stillness. The time passed, — how long I could not tell, — and again the bell clattered its emphatic command, and there followed a deep rumbling as though of distant thunder as the propeller bit the water. We were going astern. The lookout man at my side breathed a word or two of astonishment and I felt that we were turning. Again came the engine-room gong, — rat-a-tang-tang-tang-tang — tang, — and the engines paused a moment, then continued in a different strain.

"Going ahead now!" whispered the man at my side, while I waited filled with that horrid dread all sailors know, the dread of impact. But no impact came, and I marvelled dumbly at a man who could twist a ship about in this fashion, and yet again the engine-room bell rang out. The lookout man panted audibly.

"Shut your breathing!" I whispered, and the man, with a gulp, was silent. We were going full ahead, and gradually our stern way died. There came a draught upon my face and the soft, silken rustle of the parting water far down beneath me, while the lookout man and myself were stricken with the helplessness of the blind.

The stream of warm, damp air, laden with forest smells, increased against our faces. A violent splashing, from some large and startled creature, — probably an alligator, — came from our port hand, and following an old practice I gazed upward, low in the sky, knowing that the best way to see things on a dark night is never to look directly at them. We continued thus for some very long minutes and then rang down to "dead slow." The night was vast and vague and featureless; at times it seemed to close about us like velvet curtains; at others it seemed to recede unfathomably remote, and we moved in the emptiness of space. This sensation of approaching and receding is a common experience of strained eyes, and requires discrimination and experience to decide between phantom and reality. We struck some floating mass, and the lookout man and I gulped in our efforts to restrain our voices: then, unmistakeably, there loomed before and over us a great blackness. We yelled a warning in chorus as there came a rending and crashing of tree branches, and next moment the lookout man and myself were flung violently to the deck!

I was up again in an instant, only to bring my head with a nasty crack against something above me. The experience was startling, for living hands seemed to clutch me from all sides. The ship was backing away and suddenly we were free, when the captain's cool and collected tone came calmly through the night.

"All right, Grummet?" he enquired.

"Yes, sir," I replied, my hands to my singing head.

"Ship trying to climb a tree," was his smooth reply that had in it a trace of laughter, and again the engine-room bell clattered.

"If any one had told me of this," I thought, "I would have said that it was impossible. Why, he can't see the bows from the bridge, and this in a river!"

Seven times in the next hour did Captain Matthew Hawks, one of the most skilled navigators and efficient of sailors, put his ship aground, and seven times, by a miracle, we got off. Tree branches raked the forecastle-head, and the lookout man and I had a lively time, never knowing at what instant and from what direction we should be brained as though by a club. Under these conditions it was no longer humanly possible to be silent. Human intercourse was necessary between us, and what we said to each other need not be recorded against us. And then the bows took something soft and gently resisting, mounted upwards, and the ship came to a stop.

"Done it this time," came the captain's comment through the dark, "guess I'll wait for day-light."

"Guess we will," remarked the man at my side, and though his tone was low it was emphatic.

The cabin lights were turned on, and when I came aft Wilfred caught sight of me and cackled unfeelingly with merriment.

" 'Ello!" said he, "Grummet's been ashore!"

The first grey suggestion of dawn revealed us with our bows embowered in leafage, and five monkeys perched wonderingly upon the rail. This in an ocean-going ship!

"We live and learn," remarked the captain; "guess I was a child before I struck this country."

"Yo' have struck it too, Matthew," said Captain Esterkay placidly, a before-breakfast cigar between his lips. "Did yo' think this hooker was an airship?"

"And six months ago," continued Captain Hawks, "I'd 'most have cried if I had put my ship ashore. Now I am only wondering what we'll have for breakfast!"

"It's climate, sir," said I. "There are five monkeys on the forecastle-head; I should n't be surprised to find an alligator snoring in my bunk. In fact, I shan't be surprised again at anything as long as I live. Shall I be getting out a kedge astern, sir?"

The captain nodded. "The Old Man put her away and I got her off, eh, Mr. Mate?" said he, smiling. "I remember saying that in my younger days. Ah, there's breakfast."

Before sunrise the ship came off the mud with a great clatter of winches, which caused some irritation among at least a dozen alligators that had come to anchor round her bows, and we proceeded up-stream.

And the matter of alligators and game generally now attracted our attention. The country was positively swarming with life, while the forest at night was in a continuous uproar that was most impressive. Throughout that day we continued up-stream, the river becoming more narrow, but remaining extraordinarily deep and often winding most abruptly. We were now in genuinely unexplored country, which fact was not a little impressive, for we never knew what a bend in the river might reveal.

For three days we continued, and the conditions surrounding us seemed to change with every mile of progress. We were getting out of that evil valley of the Amazon, which had had an indescribable effect upon us all. The land lay no longer a stagnant swamp, but undulated with hills that grew higher and steeper in the west. After three days' journeying the captain took the ship's position, and some two hours later he blew a prolonged blast upon the whistle. Fancy pictured that strange sound, bursting for the first time upon the ears of the forest and startling the very trees. And so wild and untouched was this country that one could almost picture a combined attack upon us by an army of wild creatures amazed at our preposterous arrival. For it must be remembered that we were actually exploring in a seagoing ship.

We whistled long and painfully throughout the day at intervals and the sound must have carried far, and when we anchored that night we got the searchlight going. I think, when I was cataloguing the various conveniences of the ship, that I have spoken of this light upon the bridge. It was not, of course, a light such as is carried by men-o'-war, but was powerful enough, and one such as is carried by well-found commercial vessels to assist in loading cargo in unfrequented ports. This machine, being a deck-fitting, fell under my charge, with all the rest. But as not only man himself suffers woefully in that sinister climate of the Amazon, but all man-made things, I had come to an arrangement with Mr. McLushley, who knew all there was to know about the bad effect of tropical climates on complicated mechanisms. The result was that you could not put your hand anywhere without encountering a particularly greasy kind of grease, which was stuck about with dead or still struggling insects of all sizes and of variously poisonous natures. Therefore, though the searchlight had not been used for a long time, it was in full working order as soon as the hood was removed, its universal joints working smoothly, and with a grating, singing hiss the long shaft of cold violet-white light sprang into being. And the moving beam as it swung glittering over the forest was followed by terrific crashes or ominous silences.

All this time none of us knew what was coming or what to expect.

"This is a wicked country," remarked the captain, shooting a pillar of light up into the sky like a gigantic flagpole, to mark our position for miles round. Up went that line of light, up and up, while the flying insects flashed in it like blowing snowflakes; and then, for a time, he played it upon the forest, enjoying the consternation it caused amid that packed world of venomous and deadly life.

And before morning, and from amid that alarming darkness, the ship was hailed, hailed loudly, by an American voice!

CHAPTER X

A VOICE FROM THE DARKNESS

THE night was exceedingly dark and very hot. To southward and westward the lightning palpitated angrily, throwing into black relief the rounded tops of the trees and emphasising the pit-like blackness of the river. It might have been the cumulative effect of the climate, but, on that night in particular, I recollect feeling very vividly our remoteness and isolation from our fellows. Moreover, our departure from Maloca, our present destination, which the captain alone knew, and the problem of how in the world we were to return through such a land of enemies, gave ample food for thought. I did not know what had been in that mysterious note so picturesquely delivered from Colonel Calvin. There were times when my commander would lay his plans very fully before me, and then again there were times when I knew no more than any stoker. Still, it was obvious that we were now in actual search of the colonel, and the loss of the stipulated return cargo did not seem to worry Captain Hawks. The little ship hummed cheerfully with the sounds of human intercourse — snatches of song, whistling and laughter, that free, ready merriment that comes among men who are on good terms with one another and with life in particular. The *Martin Connor* was a happy ship. And then, in a momentary pause in the sounds aboard, and from the impenetrable darkness about us, came, without warning, a loud, strident, human voice! I shall never forget the sound of that voice or the effect it produced; coming as it did it set the nerves jangling like a peal of alarm bells, and every man that heard it did, literally, jump! It was a rasping human bellow, and of such volume and intensity as to have about it the shocking quality that voices have in dreams, or when heard while coming out from under an anæsthetic.

"For 'Evink's sake!" piped Wilfred shrilly, running out of his "Office," while Captain Hawks shot from his chair and ran to the rail.

"American ship ahoy!" came the voice.

"Ahoy! Hoy! Hoy! Hoy! Oy! Oy ..." repeated the echo in the forest.

"Hello!" yelled back Captain Hawks, and I could hear laughter in his tone, the laughter of pleasure.

"Is that the American ship that was at Maloca?" enquired that truly staggering voice.

"Yes!" answered the captain, laughing outright, "don't you recognise my voice, Ezra? There's no mistaking yours!"

"Matthew Hawks!!" was the answer, and this time, raised to its fullest pitch, that voice seemed to shake the very ship.

There was a powerful light arranged upon a gooseneck forward of the midship structure which we used when working cargo. This could be taken from its stepping, and with a length of wire could be carried about the deck, and was switched on from the bridge. I turned this on, and running down I carried the light to the side, while others threw over the ladder. Into the radius of light there shot a canoe; it slid over the water and came round with extreme dexterity to rest by the ladder. It did not arrive slowly with diminishing way; it arrived full speed and stopped dead.

"That's good!" I thought; "that takes a bit of doing."

In the canoe were five practically naked men, and the strong, uncompromising light I held shone upon their muscles, their skin having that beautiful silklike texture which the human complexion takes when permanently exposed to the open air. The man in the bow of the canoe unloaded himself with such poise and balance that the frail vessel never swayed, and he started climbing the ladder. He came up like some agile ape, and I stepped back and to one side to give room to my commander.

When Colonel Ezra Calvin arrived, and I levelled that pitiless light upon him, he presented a
picture that, for a moment, struck each and every
one dumb. He was a long, lank, gaunt New
Englander. He was cleanly shaved as though
fresh from a barber and getting rather bald
on the top of his head. Had you seen him in the
ceremonious costume of a Chinese mandarin, or
in the make-up of the Sultan of Turkey, or in
the sombre garb of a monk, or in the full-blown
kit of a British field marshal, you would still
have had no vestige of doubt that he came from
New England. And when he first burst upon our
breathless gaze like a lantern picture, his entire
costume was a sort of Masonic-apron-like arrangement of native workmanship. Yet he appeared the very heart and soul of prim respectability, and New England to the hilt!

I do not know what we expected to see, but
I do know that we did not expect what we did
see. With the exception of the captain we were
all temporarily deprived of the powers of speech.
We just stood there and gaped at the incongruity of the man and his costume. For a white
man, who has been living with savages, in some
savage costume is not startling as a rule, for he
usually takes on some subtle demeanour of the
savage. But when the white man remains a
white man and retains all the Christian virtues

and is palpably the pink of all respectability; then, when he is seen in an almost negligible native costume, you behold a concatenation of the seemingly impossible.

Captain Hawks darted forward, and those two men came as near hugging as the Anglo-Saxon will allow himself, while we, as I have said, stood and gaped. Wilfred broke the spell by retreating hurriedly with imperfectly concealed mirth. As for myself I suffered severely, but I kept a straight face, while, at the captain's introduction, Colonel Calvin shook me by the hand with the ceremonious solemnity of manner befitting a deacon of the church. Then with my commander he strode away, grave, dignified, entirely unabashed, and wholly unself-consciously naked. A sense of humour is a splendid thing, but it is trying sometimes to possess one. I went away filled to the brim with laughter, but the kind of laughter that filled me was in itself a token of respect to that extraordinary man; it was the laughter that any amazing incongruity affords, and I state most emphatically that it was not *at* the colonel, but at the humour of the circumstances.

In a very short time, Ezra Calvin was arrayed in a complete outfit of clothing, but as the garments were made originally for the captain, who, though a big man, was not so tall as the colonel, and at the same time much broader, they did not fit to perfection; but that did not matter.

On the bridge we sat for most of that night, and I do not think that I have ever been more interested. That long, angular man, with his remarkable voice now reduced to a suitable tone, talked on hour after hour to the captain, Captain Esterkay, and myself; and what he had to tell, no less than the manner of his telling it, was a rich entertainment to the listener.

He had demonstrated his remarkable personality from the first; for to appear as he had appeared, attired as he was attired amid a crowd of waiting men, all of them with but one exception total strangers, and show not by the flicker of an eyelid a trace of nervousness or embarrassment, requires no small measure of real character. There was no diffidence in the man, nor was there conceit; he was entirely sure of himself, not in a boasting, top-lofty manner, but with a placid, unworried knowledge of his own powers. Doubtless, when the Rio Maranon Company at length forced him to take to the death-haunted jungle, he had done so in a quietly merry mood, regarding it as an interesting and passing experience, when any other man would have decided that he went, inevitably, to his death. All the same, the colonel had had a very bad time, about as bad a time as even he could stand.

For nearly three months he was alone in the forest, a forest infested with terrors and reduced, even at the brightest midday, to a deep sepulchral gloom. He was lost, utterly lost, or — and he admitted it — he would willingly have given himself up after six weeks and chanced the Rio Maranon's worst. He very nearly lost his reason, and he was apparently conscious of his tottering mental faculties, for he described vividly to us his sensations at that time. It was like, so he said, slipping down the face of a slope leading to a precipice. He knew that he was going mad, and there were many days that he did not remember. The clothes that he escaped in were soon torn to ribbons, and one day, when he awoke from a period of lost memory, he found his arms and ammunition gone; and then, indeed, things looked black for him. But even then he did not despair — not quite.

The Blowgun Indians had found him lying apparently dead. The discovery, for them, must have been remarkable, for there was no indication of how he got there. Nevertheless, he was not dead, and they carried him home with them as a curiosity, and in the hands of people reputed to be implacably ferocious and cannibals to boot, his amazing constitution recovered itself bit by bit. Gradually, under the influence of rest and frequent feeding his body mended itself and his reason gained a more stable equilibrium. He no longer felt the appalling sensation of slipping downwards to the sheer drop of insanity. Weeks followed weeks and he was a long time ill, and for weeks and weeks those naked heathen nursed him in a manner no Christian could have bettered. But one need not be a Christian to be in possession of a rigorous code of honour, and the colonel found that he was as safe amid the Blowgun Indians as he would have been in New York or London; perhaps even safer, since here there was no chance of being run over or robbed as there is in any large Christian city! He was more than fed, he was positively stuffed with food, and word by word he picked up a few fragments of the Indians' speech. He could speak their language now with some ease, for he possessed the linguistic faculty. Thus he was able, before long, to explain to the Indians his precise position and they were interested. They found no difficulty in grasping what he said, for they were of a high order of intelligence. They were able to realise that he was of a tribe foreign to the white men in possession of the main Amazon stream and that he was at war with them. Being a man of wide experience gathered from all over the world, the colonel, not unnaturally, was able to be of no little use and help to the Indians; yet the New Englander made no blundering assumption of superiority. He was too wise a man to fail in realising that in a great many respects he was not the superior of the Blowguns in their native forests. He was at enormous disadvantages, disadvantages that stripped him of many of the privileges of being a white man. But he set himself to learn, and such a man in almost any community of persons would naturally rise to a position of importance. He discovered that the Indians were, without doubt, cannibals, and that they had a remarkable custom of boning heads whereby the head shrank to about the size of an apple without losing its likeness to the original owner, retaining even its expression. There were, he said, several erstwhile officials of the Rio Maranon Company thus represented, together with a German botanist and an English railroad engineer. This, and some other discoveries, must have been a considerable shock to that lonely white man amid those unknown people, but Ezra Calvin could stand shocks; he was made that way. At night, by himself, he would argue out his position, and the advisability of lodging some protest against the cannibalism, the head-boning business, and one or two other details; but, to put it in no way too strongly, his position was delicate, delicate in many ways. It seemed, as he put it whimsically enough himself, hardly good manners to inter-

fere! Driven into the wilderness by his own
colour, or by what the Indians would naturally
consider his own colour, he had been found at
the edge of death by these people, who, without thought of reward, had nursed him back to
sanity and life with the most extreme gentleness
and consideration. And they could always say,
"Well, if you do not like our ways you can go,
we won't keep you!" and the colonel, hard as he
was, had no intention of again facing the forest
alone. He did, however, at length lodge his protest; as a white man he could not do less; and
the Indians were politely interested and just a
little amused!

Split into tribes at variance with one another,
tribal conflicts were naturally not infrequent,
and upon one occasion, by the colonel's strategic
suggestions, his tribe gained an overwhelming
victory. From that moment Ezra Calvin became
a valued friend of the chief, a venerable old gentleman who had eaten many dozens of his fellow
men! So the colonel's hopes revived of weaning
these otherwise excellent people from some of
their ways and of introducing them to Christianity. He was certainly a remarkable mis-
sionary, and he threw the full force of his powerful personality into achieving this end; not with
blunt demands, mournful entreaties, or hysterical
exhortations, or by threats and a veiled superi-

ority of manner, but by suggestions of Machia-
vellian subtlety.

"I wanted to see," said the colonel, with really
grand simplicity, "if I could n't do something in
return for all that they had done for me!"

He was much too big a man to boggle over
details.

"I wanted to give 'em the Idea," said he, "and
before six months was out I was speakin' their
language pretty freely. I did n't get side-tracked
on the subject of clothing or creeds like most
missionaries do. As for clothing, I had none myself, and clothing don't make decency anyway.
Besides, if a man looks like those Indians do, I
guess he don't need no clothing to cover him up
as we do who are like some fungus that's grown
white by living covered in darkness from the
sun. Also, clothing, once you have lived without
it, is unhealthy. No, I stuck to the main point."

With tact and knowledge and supreme delicacy, with understanding sympathy and grati-
tude, the colonel set about his task undismayed.
The Indians were great lovers of ceremony and
of hero-worship. The heroic deeds of the great
ones who had departed were jealously guarded
and handed down from generation to generation,
and gradually, as their intimacy grew, the Indians, bit by bit, drew Ezra Calvin into their
inner life, acquainting him with their hopes and

beliefs. An exchange of such confidences was only natural, and so the colonel had his chance. It must be remembered that he was an extraordinary man who had, by then, — as a result of his desire, of his affection for and knowledge of these people, — gained an ascendancy over them, and knew just how, precisely, to reach them and give his words the most effect. He introduced them to Christianity through their own language, by their own ideas, by getting at their own most private point of view. Of how many missionaries, I wonder, could the same be said?

And in the end the colonel, in the main, won the day!

He won it without book or church or society to help him, sitting clothed in native fashion in their midst, and he made no fatal mistake over side issues. The cannibalism and the head-boning stopped to a very great extent, and his teaching held in other directions too.

So the months passed, and the colonel was giving up all hope of ever again seeing his kind or of reaching civilisation. While the tribe was moving from one hunting ground to another, having infrequent contact with the river Indians who feared them, they heard, at intervals and by means of the mysterious Indian "wireless," that there was a steamer in the river with a striped flag at her stern that the river Indians spoke well of. A striped flag such as was described could only be American, and a sudden hurricane of longing and homesickness smote that lonely and intrepid man. The steamer was hundreds of miles away, yet, would not an American ship help an American in such a position as was he, — who could not escape through what was practically the one road out? Moreover, while living with the Indians he had made a discovery that had positively taken his breath away, and I have already said that he was a man who could stand shocks. So he resolved to try and in some way come in touch with the steamer with the striped flag, and his copper-skinned friends were willing enough to help him. The results of these combined efforts were already known to us.

Apart from his personal idiosyncrasies, Colonel Ezra Calvin was not unlike the great tribe of wanderers that one comes across in odd corners of the globe. They are to be found usually beyond the edge of civilisation, possessed by an ungovernable restlessness and a spirit of romance. They have no vices, these unofficial explorers, and they combine an extraordinary number of diverse abilities without either the will or the desire to turn them to any great material profit. They pass from country to country and are of all nationalities, though they are usually either American or British. They are never seemingly in want of money and always appear to have enough for their simple needs. They die, as like as not, in some foreign hospital of some obscure tropical ailment and leave nothing but a battered trunk or two behind them. They invariably talk well and easily, and their vocabulary embraces technical and other phrases in half a dozen languages and dialects in which there is a strong flavouring of the sea. They are patriotic and love their country, but they never live in it, and they enjoy a surprising grasp of world politics. They have no relations and few friends and no real desire for either. They are, in fact, detached eccentrics, capable of the most appalling hardships, and though full of amazing schemes they are wholly without a plan in life. They feel no vestige of alarm at any crisis, and would show no dismay at being stranded without money in New York, Liverpool, or any other place, and they would somehow get money, and get it honestly. Their clothing is generally vaguely remarkable, comprising, as likely as not, a suit purchased in Kansas or it might be Glasgow, a shirt bought in Hongkong, shoes from Budapest, and a hat acquired in Simla by means of a bet. They can name all the principal lighthouses, bar-rooms, and mountain peaks in the world, and they have met and conversed intimately with South and Central American presidents, Zulu chiefs, great explorers, American millionaires, English lords, and the lesser German nobility. They are casehardened to all shocks, they know the inside history of many an unlawful deal, and they are usually aiming for some place which you would go far to avoid.

To such a tribe belonged Colonel Ezra Calvin, though he had, in addition to his tribal marks, his own startling personality. As a prospector for hidden wealth in almost inaccessible places he would have been hard to beat; it was only in the matter of diplomatic negotiations with the all-powerful Rio Maranon Company that he had failed; but then the real out-and-out, concentrated American never has been a diplomatist, though it remains to be seen in the very near future if he will be! There had been no diplomatic necessity in his dealings with the Blowgun Indians, for his relations with his rescuers had been of the most cordial nature. As an exploring partner of such a shipmaster and owner as Captain Hawks, Colonel Calvin was indispensable. But there could be no doubt at all that the colonel's difficulty with the Rio Maranon Company, when added to ours, was, metaphorically speaking, enough to sink the ship, and, speaking practically, enough to make it next thing to the impossible for us to leave the country without international negotiations.

The captain had written to the American Consul at Para, informing him fully on all details concerning Massingbird's death, together with the signed declarations of the three witnesses of that event, and explaining that we should be back in Para within a few months ready to answer all questions, and, in fact, put ourselves entirely in the hands of the authorities — at Para; but not in the hands of the paid authorities of the Rio Maranon Rubber Company. This the captain had done upon the advice of the British Agent at Manaos, and also following that advice we had departed hurriedly from Manaos, and the Rio Maranon Company had unsuccessfully endeavoured to arrest me at Maloca. How that endeavour failed I have already described, together with the failure to arrest the ship, while the details incidental to those failures were not likely to better our case. So the Rio Maranon Company held, as it were, a very long bill against us, and when it became known that we had Colonel Calvin aboard, — Colonel Calvin who had (1) refused with considerable directness at Serpa to give an account of himself; (2) slipped through its toils at Manaos; (3) at some point, not indicated, deliberately run down a Rio Maranon launch when the officials therein had demanded his papers; and (4) who was now wanted "alive or dead" by the Rio Maranon Company, which alleged that he was inciting the Indians to revolt (which was a lie), and who had come openly into competition with that company, — and when it became known that we had every intention of taking the colonel out of the country with us, it was obvious that the Rio Maranon Rubber Company, which owned the lives of a great many men, and which was responsible for the deaths of a great many more, would make no half-hearted effort to prevent us from escaping down the one and only road which we could use, namely, the Amazon River.

Captain Hawks had already given me some indication of what he intended to do in the event of certain complications which had now come about; he had suggested his probable line of action before we sailed, when we were lying at anchor in Galveston Bay. Captain Hawks was not, I must admit, all that he should have been (who is?); but, on the other hand, it is an ethical problem that is altogether beyond me as to whether he was right or wrong in his intention to trade honourably with the original inhabitants of a vast country which is claimed by four independent states and a commercial trust, none of which either governs, surveys, improves, or even polices the land they all squabble over.

At any rate, his intention held good. In our hold were the trade goods purchased by and belonging to Captain Matthew Hawks, though at the time we loaded them he had no idea that it would be with the mysterious Blowgun Indians that we should do business. Yet had he seen at that time all the difficulties awaiting us, and all the difficulties then surrounding his lost partner, bold man though he was I think he might have hesitated — though perhaps not for long — to add to them by proceeding dead against the expressed wishes of five dog-in-the-manger opponents such as Peru, Colombia, Ecuador, Brazil, and a ruthless commercial combine such as the Rio Maranon Rubber Company. But he had had no idea of such a return cargo as had been intimated in Colonel Calvin's mysteriously delivered note! All the same, the situation was, in popular parlance, a very tall proposition for one small cargo boat to meet. But she was a tough little cargo boat all the same!

The colonel's bodyguard of Indians were entertained upon the forward main-deck by our crew, who were supplied with the means of entertainment. The difficulties of speech were no real barriers, for extreme amiability characterised the meeting, — amiability tempered with marked respect upon both sides. Ten other canoes also came alongside, each canoe carrying a crew of six magnificent men. They left their blowguns in their canoes, moored to the bottom of the ladder, as a token of trust and general politeness, much as a policeman might remove his helmet when entering the house of a friend. That our crew and the Blowgun Indians would be friends was likely, for both were real proper men, though widely different in race. There was little of "Lo the poor Indian!" in these spare and elegant savages, who could kill you in dead silence with a puff of breath. They had, practically speaking, never come in contact with white men before, and white men had never come in contact with them — and lived afterwards! They were therefore entirely unspoiled, untouched, unchanged, and there was not a man among us who did not realise that it was an extraordinary experience. In the wild parts of the world, equality and inequality between people are measured in terms of force and power, and not by intellectual achievement except in so much as intellectual achievement bestows power in the shape of firearms, or, in other words, the power to kill. And with regard to this last consideration there was little doubt that we were even or nearly so; any advantage lying with the Indians and not with us. We might, and perhaps could, defy four South American states and the Rio Maranon Company, but there was no doubt at all that we could not defy the Blowgun Indians! I moved about among our men with watchful eyes, and put the nature of our surroundings very emphatically to them. On no account whatever, and for no reason, must there be any trouble. It was true that the colonel had much power with them, and that our reputation with the Indians was first class, but if a quarrel were to arise, tough ship's company though they might be, we should inevitably cease to exist, and the manner of our exit made one shudder to contemplate. But there was never any suggestion of trouble, for everything was nice and friendly.

The leader of the Indians who had accompanied the colonel was not the chief, but a sort of secretary for foreign affairs. We could not begin to pronounce his name, but Wilfred promptly christened him "Alf," and so, to us, Alf he remained. The little cook possessed an obscure and subtle ability for giving people and things names which, though seemingly illogical, yet stuck by their very incongruity. Thus the alligator that occupied much valuable space on the after main-deck was always referred to quite gravely as "Percy" by us all, including the captain and Mr. McLushley. That fourteen-foot monstrosity, by the way, if not exactly a pet, was becoming resigned to his captivity; a captivity brightened by a large and regular supply of food.

Alf was truly a magnificent specimen, standing a good six feet one and with a slim and graceful carriage that was a joy to behold. He was a light sort of copper-bronze in hue with an unblemished skin. As Wilfred said: "Yer don't need no clothes when you 'ave a body like our friend Alf's." Alf's face was oblong, not squat and Mongolian, with clean-cut features stamped with the marks of intelligence and a good clean stock of forefathers. Had his colouring been white he would have made an extraordinarily good example of our race, yet with an added quality that would have made men fear him in no uncertain manner. This quality I could put no name to, though I was aware of its presence in all, or almost all, the Blowgun Indians. It was an unknown, unplumbed abyss, and to use a metaphor, was like an *un*moral and noble criminality. You felt that with all his real excellence, Alf would, on certain occasions, logical enough to him, but incomprehensible to you, do shocking and awful things as a matter of course. If, for instance, you fought him and you put up a real good fight, and if he killed you, as he would with his blowgun, he would be tempted to eat you as a sort of token of *respect* to your departed spirit.

Well, there it was; there was no possibility of getting that point of view, so it was no good trying; it had to be accepted as one of the multitude of mysteries that surround us in a primeval forest of pagan America or in the crowded streets of a Christian city.

I conducted Alf over the ship and we were very polite to each other, you may be sure. He was quite able to grasp the general idea of the vessel's construction, though iron and steel were new to him. Still, he realised that given such metals and the power to work them, such a form of gigantic canoe might be made, but he could not in the least understand the engines, which last Mr. McLushley himself endeavoured to explain by sign and action. Alf and the chief engineer regarded each other impassively for a moment, looking each other up and down and finally unflinchingly in the eyes — a long, searching stare; then they nodded with complete gravity as though each were saying to himself: "Verily, here is a Man!" But the principles that govern reciprocating machinery not unnaturally were beyond Alf. He was a little dazed and astonished, though in no way alarmed, by the slow and delicately ponderous, calculated, and ordained precision of movement that answered, so exactly, Mr. McLushley's battered and capable hands upon the little black wheel projecting from the large copper pipe that held in slavery that vast array of gleaming metal. He caught on to the fact that what he beheld was not magic but a man-made thing, and suddenly turning to us as representatives of the race that could create such things, he made a movement that was a gesture of respect that was superb in its simple dignity; it made one blush!

So the night passed, full of interest and events, in a social function that could only be called profoundly odd. It was as though here, far beyond the boundaries of the white man's influence and activity, we were received and measured at the very entrance of the unknown by the unknown inhabitants.

The following day, the *Martin Connor*, that essential product of science and commerce, with her electric light, multitubular boiler, her automatic ash ejector and Kelvin compass, plastered with insurance policies and legal agreements, continued into the strange domain whose inhabitants, as strange and as unknown as their country, had, as it were, examined us and permitted us to enter!

CHAPTER XI

THE GREAT DISCOVERY

As soon as daylight permitted we were under weigh next morning, to the vast interest of the Blowgun Indians, who for some mysterious reason seemed to find humour in the proceeding! Alf and his party remained on board, and we hoisted on deck their canoe (a long and elegant craft dug out from a single tree-trunk and shaved to a thinness of sheet tin, then scraped and polished until it had an outward surface not unlike that of a meerschaum pipe). The steam capstan startled them; they thought, and not unnaturally, that we must have a gang of men they had not seen concealed beneath the deck. We managed to assure them, however, that this was not so, and we took some trouble in the matter; for we had every intention of remaining upon the best possible terms with these people and their terrible weapon.

It now became obvious that we were entering a country that was altogether different from the Amazon lowlands. This change, strictly speaking, began somewhere about Maloca, but in that place the change had been very gradual. Now, every hour of steaming marked a difference.

The current of the river grew quicker, the banks became higher and were often of a rocky nature. The swamps seemed left behind us, and there arose to the north and west a range of hills that were bare of trees toward the top. The climate also improved. The heat was less, and to our great thankfulness the insects were no longer in such uncounted millions. Occasionally the river narrowed into a rocky gorge, and to take a sea-going ship up such an uncharted stream was no child's play. The colonel, however, with his inde-fatigable industry, had taken soundings, and we kept two men busy with the lead. The river, you must understand, was still a big river accord-ing to our standards, but was just a creek in com-parison with the Amazon. Captain Hawks kept on at full speed in order that he might have the greatest possible command of the ship, though had we run aground then upon the rocks that fringed the banks we, or rather the ship, would have stayed there for all time. The colonel knew the river, so did the Indians, and the men with the lead were busy on either side of the bridge-deck. But to take accurate soundings from a swiftly moving ship in a swiftly flowing river is impossible, and it was, at best, but guesswork. But from the manner in which the line ran out it was possible to form some opinion of the water beneath us.

Here and there great masses of rock rose above the forest trees draped in festoons of fern-like plants, and occasionally an open glade showed up amid the trees. This was beautiful country and enchanting to the eye sickened of extra-tropical regions. And the forest swarmed with life. Droves, or perhaps I should say flocks, of monkeys went sailing through the trees with a rapidity and ease that suggested the flight of birds, and their passage was accompanied by an immense chatteration. The hour for the midday meal went unnoticed. Every man who could be was on deck gazing upon a country which, with the exception of the colonel, had, in all probability, never been seen before by white men. Moreover, the risks and dangers of our progress were manifest to all, for it was rather like riding a bicycle up a wheel track of a waggon; and only the most prompt and immediate obedience of all saved the ship from disaster several times that day. When we anchored again that night a sigh of relief went up from us all, including the captain, who had never left the bridge since dawn.

For three days of intense vigilance we continued, and by then the nature of the country had altered very greatly. Mountains — real mountains — rose high in the north and west, unnamed, unknown, and unexplored, for we were too far south for any of the trails that led over the Andes and into the Amazon Basin. The improvement in the climate was welcome to us all, and though possibly a few months before we should have considered it unbearably humid, it was, by comparison with what we had been in, almost temperate. The trees also changed, and we saw many species we had not seen before; and though, no doubt, they all had names, I am afraid that we did not know them. The river divided at a series of rocky islands, and then branched off, and obeying the colonel's instructions we followed the northerly branch through a fine gorge of red rock that glistened with hundreds of minute waterfalls that fell like rain through a tangle of drooping ferns. Later, in the early afternoon the gorge ceased abruptly and gave place to a mile or two of low-lying lands; farther on the banks receded and we entered a wide, deep lake.

We were now some sixteen hundred miles inland from the Atlantic, and were, as a matter of fact, considerably nearer the Pacific. Though various statements are made concerning the distance which ocean-going ships can ascend the Amazon, from our experience I am inclined to think that some of the statements are travellers' tales. The main stream is said to be navigable for seagoing ships as far as Iquitos in Peru, about twenty-three hundred miles from the Atlantic, while vessels of a less draught, but drawing fourteen feet, can go as far as Achual Point, which is four hundred and eighty-six miles beyond Iquitos. Beyond Achual Point the stream is considered dangerous, though I saw myself some steamers at Para intended for the navigation of the stream above Achual Point, and they must have drawn at least eight feet, though they were bound for Pongo de Manseriche, which is many, many miles beyond Achual Point. Therefore, in comparison with these figures our distance inland did not sound so much, though actually, and when studying the chart, I remember that we seemed a tremendously long way from the sea. As Wilfred said, "It seemed a long, long way to Tipperary"; and then the sudden discovery of this great sheet of water which we entered that afternoon was, considering our position, quite startling. The shore lines stretched away upon either hand until they became thin ribbons in the distance, as do the beaches of an atoll appear to a ship entering a South Sea lagoon. But beyond the shore the land rose high and distant. In places the surface of the lake was clotted with forest wreckage woven together into floating islands and populous with life.

"Could n't find a better place to strip a blade," remarked the captain, and rang off the engines to "dead slow" and then to "stop," allowing our impetus to carry us a full mile, winding in and out amid those floating islands.

I was standing on the forecastle-head with Wilfred at my side. Suddenly the little cook shot out a thin arm and pointed ahead, while astonishment robbed him of speech. High above the mountains to westward, at a great distance, and at a positively staggering altitude, ethereal and fairy-like in the sky, stood the faint outline of a gigantic range of mountains. The mountains beyond the shore line had appeared high until that moment, and undoubtedly they were high, but the vastness of that ethereal range beyond — so distant that the summits seemed to be severed from the earth, and yet, in spite of their manifest distance so high, appearing thus mysterious and remote — was, literally, thrilling and dramatic. The sight was, as the saying is, enough to take one's breath away, and one's astonishment was in no way lessened by the thought that here, indeed, were the Andes, seen from the *east*, and from an ocean-going ship! At that moment the bridge also caught sight of them.

"Look ahead, Grummet! In the sky!" came Captain Hawks's voice quickly.

"I have just this moment seen them, sir!" I answered; and the captain laughed and waved his arms in a gesture more expressive than words.

"What next, I wonder!" he said.

It was only for a moment or two that that line of mountains remained visible, during some chance balance of lighting; then they faded and were not, leaving upon the mind of the beholder an impression of something wholly unearthly, and of something tremendously solemn. I had never expected to see the Andes from the east. Viewed from the west their whole extent is often seen; but their eastern slopes are usually accounted too gradual in character, and the crests do not therefore appear until many thousand feet have first been climbed. But there are great portions of that continent that are still unknown, where unknown sights may meet the eye of the traveller; and certainly, from one place at least, those great mountains, the second highest in the world, can be seen from the east in their entirety, for we saw them. However, we never saw them again that way, though six men saw them at the same moment, six men whose eyesight was not only of the best, but trained and used to long distances. Therefore, and as we were in a wholly unexplored region, I have not the least doubt that it was, indeed, the Andes we saw, vast and remote, revealed for one extraordinary moment by some chance of sunlight, and I, for one, shall never forget the experience.

By using what open spaces there were in that large inland lake, and by nosing our way upon impetus through the slush of forest débris, Captain Hawks got the ship across the ten or fifteen miles to the opposite shore, while multitudes of birds rose circling in alarm at our passage. The trees fringing the western side of the lake came into view with rapidly rising ground behind them. Continually sounding, we got across the lake, and, as we approached the shore, there came gradually upon the ear a whisper that grew more distinct as we progressed. It puzzled us upon the forecastle-head for some time until the sound, growing more pronounced, became finally the sustained roar of falling water.

With infinite caution, and with all the knowledge and apparatus of a ship making a landfall off an unknown seacoast, we approached and dropped anchor at nightfall. After watching the iron fall clear and hauling short, I leaned on the rail a moment and looked round, and in one silent minute there were half a hundred canoes about us, appearing as mysteriously as they had appeared at Maloca. I do not know how it was done; it was uncanny in the extreme, and was as though they had risen from beneath the surface. Of course the light was fading, as it had been at Maloca, and of course there were many floating islands and masses of forest wreckage surrounding us and behind which, in the dusk, a canoe full of men, if perfectly motionless, could hide. Yet there was clear water about us for several hundred yards, and it was in this clear water that the canoes seemed to make their first appearance. And as each canoe was full of the deadly Blowgun Indians, the sight, even though they were friendlily disposed toward us, was sufficiently impressive. This was woodcraft of a superior kind, and being aquatic in character earned our profound respect. Alf, upon the main-deck, greeted his brethren with a guttural cry, and at once the silence was broken by a cheerful uproar, and the canoes came sweeping alongside. Every man had with him his eight-foot blowgun, while slung at his hip was a gourd containing his terrible ammunition. The Indians were invited aboard, and they came in crowds, and upon both sides an attitude of affable friendliness and respect prevailed. For the ship must have been full of the unknown and possibly dangerous unexpected to the Indians, while we, outnumbered twenty to one, had no intention of being otherwise than most polite. The fear of death was therefore not absent from all our minds, Indians and whites alike, and the fear of death promotes good manners in a way not realised in a civilisation where you can be as rude as you like and only be imprisoned or fined.

That night was somewhat extraordinary. The ship positively swarmed with Indians, mostly of

a magnificent physique and wholly untouched by
any previous intercourse with white men. Their
shocking reputation also added to the strangeness of the situation, and even Wilfred carried
himself with a certain reserve and caution. As
for myself, I will admit at once that I was scared.
No man who was not a fool could be otherwise.
The Indians clustered and jostled at the galley
door, where Wilfred explained, by the medium of
signs, the mysteries of the white man's cooking
apparatus. They hesitated to enter doorways,
and would peer in at one unexpectedly with
friendly faces that yet bore the obvious possibilities of an expression of the greatest ferocity.
I got some considerable shocks that night! With
the fittings and appurtenances of the ship they
displayed the happiest interest not wholly devoid
of fear, and the ship, being, as she was, such a collection of strange and wonderful contrivances,
kept them in a subdued mood that in time wore
off. That there should be a live alligator in a sort
of gigantic pig-pen on the after deck excited their
mirth, though Stadger, Wilfred's acquired dog,
and one of the most amiable of the ship's company, struck fear in their hearts, for he was a
wholly strange animal. They thought that 'Arry
Ketchold must be commander on account of his
size, and with all simplicity they dismissed the
engines and the electric light as miracles beyond

their grasp, and which only these pale faced men from a far distant tribe could possibly understand or manage. The iron of which the ship was constructed appeared to be most wonderful of all, and in consequence of this, a surprise which the captain was holding in store for us all came before he had intended it. Wilfred was the accidental medium.

After some hours had been consumed in exploring the ship and in affable interchange, our crew opened up negotiations for trade, and in a short time a brisk business was in progress. Some time after midnight the Indians departed, leaving behind them a surprising medley of things, but not, however, one blowgun or set of darts! I could not help but regard this fact as somewhat significant. But the crew were pleased and so were the Indians, which, after all, was all that mattered, for to establish pleasant social and business relations with these people was what the captain wished. Wilfred had also been trading, and he had not confined his operations to what is termed "curios" or "junk." While we were at a late supper the little man marched in, and with the light of a great emotion in his bright eyes he planted down with a thump in the middle of the table a granite-iron (I think it is called) saucepan filled with smooth, water-worn, bean-shaped pebbles of pure gold that varied in size from that

of a pea to almost a pigeon's egg! When I say
that this saucepan was filled with nuggets I mean
that it was full to overflowing, much as though
its contents had been shingle scooped up from
a beach. Moreover, this gold was in realisable
form; to the most inexpert it was obviously gold,
not partially hidden in dull lumps of un-
crushed, ore-bearing rock, but smooth, shining,
and yellow, like a five-dollar gold-piece or an
English sovereign. To Timothy Hanks and myself, who knew nothing of this surprise which the
captain and the colonel had in store for us, and
even to Captain Esterkay, who only knew of the
reported presence of gold in this unknown country, the sight of that ordinary cooking utensil with
its most extraordinary contents was as startling
as so much lyddite attached to a burning fuse.

Captain Hawks smiled and glanced keenly up
at Wilfred and asked: —

"Whose?"

"Yours," replied Wilfred promptly, with a
bird-like briskness of manner.

"Explain," said Captain Hawks, still smiling.

"Sut'nly. A little while ago, when them Hin-
dians come round to my galley, I noticed one
old gent dressed in a pair of fine, pure gold hear-
rings. So, when the others had gone on to look
at something helse, I kep 'im, accidental, sort of,
talkin' by means of signs, you know. 'E says to

me, in signs, "'Ow much d' you want for that theer knife?' pointin' to one of them three big knives what I cut up fresh meat wiv. I'd seen 'is hear-rings some time back an' I hintermated to 'im, like, that 'e could 'ave the knife fer a pebble or two like what 'e was wearin' in place of a full suit of clothes. 'E seemed to think me soft in the 'ead, but I did n't mind thet, an' orf 'e goes an' comes back presently in 'is canoe with that little lot" (nodding at the saucepan on the table) "in one of them theer jourds. When I see what 'e 'ad brought I was generous-like. 'You can 'ave three knives,' I says, in signs, at the same time ketchin' 'old of the jourd, not snetchin', y' know, but jest takin' it perlite-like wivout hundue waste o' time. I give 'im the three knives an' hempties the jourd into the fust thing as come 'andy, which was thet theer saucep'n. The three knives belonged to the ship, the ship belongs to you, therefore the gold is yours!"

Captain Hawks grinned.

"Wilfred," said he, "Cert'nly Wilfred."

"Yus, sir?"

"Wilfred Gee, old friend."

"Thet's me, Capting 'Auks."

"I make you a present of those three knives, and, in consequence, the gold is yours."

"Mine!" gasped the little man, "mother, what 'll I do wiv it!"

"I'll lock it in the safe for you," replied the captain, "for, at a conservative estimate, there are many thousand dollars which any bank in the United States would hand you across the counter in exchange. You might even retire from the sea, if you wished."

"But I don't want to retire from the sea, least-ways not from this ship. Are you givin' me an intimation of the noble horder of the sack? Are you givin' me the boot? In pline Henglish, are you droppin' the noddle on my boko?"

"Come again," said the captain; "what d' you mean?"

"Well, it sounds as if you was dischargin' me, or as if you was tellin' me as 'ow I could go at the end of the cruise."

"Don't be an all-fired jackass. I'm giving you many thousand dollars," said the captain, still grinning; and Wilfred stared at him.

"It's unusual," said the cook.

"Admitted," remarked the captain; "but we are in an unusual place. Are you too proud to take it from me?"

"Of course I'm not, if you reely mean it," answered Wilfred, still eyeing the captain intently. "'Ad n't you better leave it till the morning?"

"D' you think I'm drunk?" asked Captain Hawks.

"Well — I — I — not what *I'd* call drunk, but careless-like."

The captain's grin grew until he threw back his head and laughed.

"Have you ever seen me drunk?" he asked finally.

"No; but I 'ave n't never seen you give away a pot o' money like so much pebbles on the beach."

"True," agreed the captain; "I guess I'd better explain."

"Guess you 'ad," said Wilfred.

Captain Hawks turned to us, and though his remarks were addressed to all, his eyes rested upon me, for he and I and Wilfred had been together since he had taken his first command, and it had been a long record of mutual struggle and friendship.

"I guess," said he, "that this will be my last cruise. The explanation is simple. The explanation of why I left Maloca without putting up any kind of fight, either with the Rio Maranon or for my return cargo of rubber, is also simple. The reasons for my actions were consequent upon that letter I got from Colonel Calvin, which told me that I could save him by coming up-stream a certain distance. There was also news in his letter of this gold. Who owns this country I can't say, though I'm inclined to think the owners are the Blowgun Indians, who are ready and prepared to trade. The goods that I can supply them with are cheap and common enough with us, but, until we came, were unobtainable for the Indians, and I guess the worth of a thing is just according to how you can get it. It has just been demonstrated that three knives, worth about four dollars each in the United States, are worth that pot of gold at the back of the Amazon because the inhabitants have more gold than knives. Sound economy, I think. Gentlemen, the reason why this will probably be my last cruise and your last cruise is, that, provided we manage to get out of the country, we shall all be very wealthy men."

There was a moment's silence during which Cert'nly Wilfred sat down heavily (for him) in the nearest chair.

"Well, an' I don't think so much of the prospec', neither," remarked the cook; "who wants to be very wealthy?"

"Wait and see," said the captain. "It may be said," he continued, "that I am poaching. But I think that would be incorrect. Poaching necessarily implies preservation in some form, and I need not remind you that there is no preservation of any kind going on here. This is disputed territory. It is quite unexplored, quite uncontrolled, and, to my thinking, still belongs to the original inhabitants whom it pleased God to put here. Now these people have any quantity of pure, alluvial gold. They don't have to dig for it, or blast for it, or crush it when found. It comes from reefs somewhere in the lower Andes, and all they have to do is to pick it up out of stream beds. It is of little use to them, because it is too soft for most purposes for which metal is employed. They use it for ornaments, but, as far as I can find out from Colonel Calvin, I gather that its cheapness renders it a poor sort of ornamentation, and it is, in fact, regarded by these Indians much as we regard a celluloid collar! Any sort of mining operations in this country is impossible, and until the alluvial gold has been removed is unnecessary. It is only by a strange and unusual set of circumstances that we are here, living unharmed amid these Indians that even the Rio Maranon Company dare not take on, which fact, incidentally, guarantees our safety for the time being from our friends in the rubber business. So, gentlemen, now is our chance. Here are we in a full-powered steamship with a good supply of trade goods that I invested in for trading purposes; only, when I did so, it was rubber I was after, not saucepans full of practically pure gold. I will, later on, draw up a system of mutual profit, a system that shall be based upon business principles according to service rendered."

Again there followed a silence which was due to the simple reason that nobody knew what to say.

For my own part I found myself unexpectedly unmoved before the prospect of probable wealth. Sailors, almost without exception, are not money-makers. This is due to a great many reasons, though principally because their energies and character take other lines, and the average sailor is simple in his wants, requiring only the necessities for decent human existence. Thus I found it with myself; I required a pleasant habitation, and I had it; palatable food, and I had it; decent raiment, which I already possessed; good tobacco, which I also possessed; and enough money to spend on necessary recreation, and this I had too. I was not at all sure that I wanted to retire from the sea, since I was as sure as one can be of anything on this earth of a pleasant ship and an old friend as commander. I discovered Captain Hawks gazing at me with a whimsical smile, and somewhat guiltily I assumed a brighter expression and glanced at Wilfred, who, in defiance of all etiquette, still sat in a cabin chair. The little man's attitude and expression depicted solemn preoccupation.

"Well, sir," said Timothy Hanks, "for myself, I am deeply grateful."

I hastily echoed these sentiments, while Captain Esterkay glided in, as it were, with a neat and courteous speech.

"I 'll found a horphanage," said Wilfred, — "sailor's horphanage with pictures on the wall!"

CHAPTER XII

DISAPPEARANCE OF CAPTAIN HAWKS

To those who have never experienced a walk through a tropical jungle, it is almost impossible to convey any adequate picture of an Amazon forest. There were one or two Indian trails leading up from the shores of the lake to the hidden waterfall that had at first puzzled us with its sound. Upon either side and above the head the verdure was compact and impenetrable; the trail was not unlike a tunnel bored through solid rock, and was almost as dark. On a full blazing noon-day the light was here reduced to the darkness of evening, though once through the undergrowth that fringed the lake the trail entered the forest proper, where a deep, church-like gloom prevailed. On all sides, and as far as it was possible to see, the great tree-trunks rose in regiments bearing aloft a thatch of green so close and interwoven as to permit no ray of sunlight to enter. The sound of the frequent deluges of tepid rain crashing downwards in a long-sustained roar was startling, while the knowledge that upon all sides one might come upon sudden and swift danger in animal or reptilian form kept one keenly upon the alert. Thus, even upon the most casual expedition one carried a gun as a matter of course. The forest thinned in places, and these areas of light attracted the eye and steps, but for the most part the gloom was even in its sombre intensity, and would, I felt sure, have driven me to insanity in a very short time.

One of my first visits ashore was to the Indian village, and I went there with Wilfred, who, with the mysterious power some men have, was already upon the best of terms with the inhabitants, and most particularly with the children. The village was in a clearing and pleasantly scented with wood smoke. The "houses" were but thatched roofs of palm raised upon bare poles, with a complete and innocent lack of privacy. Our arrival was the signal for a general stampede of copper-skinned youngsters, who came shrieking and laughing toward us, while their mothers, busy over domestic matters, called peremptory orders to their offspring, who paid not the least attention. And this total lack of fear in the children for strange men of another race spoke eloquently, so I thought, of the formidable weapon which their parents used with such deadly skill! Wilfred had come armed with sugar candies of his own perfect manufacture, and these he threw into the air, the children, with immense chatteration and glee, catching them in their little brown fists, as pretty a sight as one could wish to see. Some were only staggering toddlers, others were long-limbed as deer, and upon them all was stamped the signs of a free independence — the independence of the blowgun. And when the candy was consumed, we moved about festooned with children, who found us a great joke. These were happy people, splendidly naked and purely unashamed; here was law, order, and decency — I was glad for ourselves that they could not see any slum in New York or London!

I discovered that an interchange of ideas was possible by means of signs, and was thus shown many matters of interest by the few men who happened to be about while Wilfred played with the children. Among other things I was spellbound by a sight of the blowgun in action. I explained my desire in this direction, and a man took me a little way into the forest carrying his blowgun, which he first, with a polite gesture, gave me into my hands to examine. The darts he also showed me, but these I examined only outwardly, and I did not remove them from the small gourd which was slung upon his hip. We had not long to wait before a drove of monkeys came flying through the upper branches, and the Indian delicately inserted a dart into the mouthpiece of his blowgun, raised the weapon, and with

the same casual aim that an expert with a revolver or rifle seems to take, he blew a sharp
breath into the gun, rather after the manner of
a man sounding a sharp staccato note upon a
coach horn. The monkeys passed on, and we followed, and in less than half a minute one of
them fell and was quickly dispatched by the
Indian, who carried it home for dinner, for
deadly as the *curare* is it is harmless as milk
unless the skin is broken. All the same, I would
not have eaten that monkey, though I was glad
that his poor little life had not been sacrificed
purely for my curiosity. But the sight of that
blowgun in action brought home very vividly our
peculiar position. To walk about unharmed amid
these remote people had an exhilarating effect
upon the nerves that is hard to describe.

As soon as it became definitely known that
we had axes, knives, machetes, brightly painted
calico, looking-glasses, tobacco of a new sort (the
Indians smoked a wild tobacco), beads, nails,
and some carpenter's tools, a great assortment
of small glittering objects such as the trimmings
used on Christmas trees, together with needles
and thread, and that we had these things ready
to exchange for the golden nuggets and float-
gold, the market opened in a brisk and lively
fashion. But the most valued of all, and that
which exchanged readily for the most gold, was

HE BLEW A SHARP BREATH INTO THE GUN

a phonograph with a dozen records. This instrument of torture actually fetched (at a rough estimate) between seven and eight thousand dollars worth of gold out of the hidden stream beds of that extraordinary country! The scenes on board the *Martin Connor* were startling and full of humour. We had stumbled, by accident, upon an inequality in the value of a scarce metal, and we brought undreamt-of delights that were as common to us as the gold was to the Indians. The situation was so essentially bizarre, fantastic, and extravagant that no one, not even the captain, could remain wholly normal or restrained. We were making our fortunes in a fairy-story manner while dealing with an unknown race of people, and while handling the commonest and most mundane of articles. Thus the temptation to what might be described as "playing the fool" was often too great to be resisted, especially with such natural-born humourists as Wilfred and Captain Esterkay to lead the way. We did a most tremendous business, a business to turn giddy the most experienced wheat operator in all the world, and this upon the iron decks of a cargo steamer at anchor amid alligators in an unmapped lake in a vast and terrible, unknown country.

It was at this time that Wilfred and I began a series of wandering investigations that were the outcome of curiosity and not in the least due to any desire to kill. The fresh-meat supply was most adequately attended to by Timothy Hanks, and in our explorations of the forest there was no necessity for Wilfred or myself to carry arms except for self-defence. Armed with machetes and repeating shotguns we spent many hours together, speaking seldom, moving slowly, and in any direction which fancy directed. When we seated ourselves and remained motionless for a short time, the strange creatures that swarmed in the jungle that was so unknown to man would continue their ordinary life to our intense interest and occasional alarm. For it is amazing how oblivious to man a really wild animal is so long as a man is to leeward and motionless. After many experiments in photography, Wilfred was forced to leave his camera behind, for the slightest movement and the click of the shutter would either frighten the game or endanger ourselves, while the gloom of the forest rendered any instantaneous work practically impossible with an ordinary camera.

This crowded mass of life was astounding. Used as we were to the man-trodden lands, this plenitude of creatures, living lives of intense activity and dying almost invariably violent deaths, was very extraordinary. Violence was the predominant note. In the fantastic glades, often draped with priceless orchids, there was continual activity and poignant tragedy in an unending struggle for existence. This will to live, this insistence of mysterious forces amid such difficulty and against such continual treachery and violence, was bewildering and in some ways rather shocking.

Along the shores of the lake we found water and semi-water dwellers that scuttled, ran, splashed, dived, or stood ready for battle according to their natures, and Wilfred and I trod warily. On the higher ground was another world of life, and I could not give the names of the creatures as we discovered them, or as they discovered us, in rotation, for I was never one to keep a journal, the ship's official log amply satisfying any natural tendency I had at that time for recording things on paper. Timothy Hanks, on the other hand, kept a most minute diary bristling with scientific names which he was at pains to acquire, and to Hanks I am indebted that I can put a handle to the odd beasts that we saw.

One day, seated upon a fallen tree, we beheld a creature that was entirely new to us both. It was about twenty inches long including a six-inch tail, and it had the appearance of a gigantic armour-plated rat. It came titupping along quite unsuspectingly down an open glade in the forest, preoccupied with daily affairs, and with the manner of a man who has just comfortable time to catch a train. He disregarded us altogether, for we remained without moving and he passed to windward of us, a compact, competent-looking animal that knew his way about. He was, so we afterwards found out, an armadillo. Monkeys there were in crowds. They came flying through the upper stories of the forest with the rapidity of birds, and when they chose, their progress was incredibly silent, while at other times they came crashing along with shouts and chatteration like a lot of children let out of school. Their agility was startling and miraculous. Their leaps through the air gave the lie direct to the theory of gravity, and defied even Wilfred's vocabulary of ejaculation. They would sail through space in a line as direct and accurate as that of an arrow, or they would drop down and down like a stone, and while you watched with growing alarm for the monkey's safety, his line of direction would change in a twinkle, and by means of a dextrous, perfectly calculated clutch at a branch, he would be off again at an acute angle to his former course. And the swaggering ease, born of long practice, which accompanied these evolutions, was comic to see. As Wilfred said: "They done that before."

Then there was a tree-climbing porcupine with

a long tail, the whole beast being about three and a half feet long. He showed not the least alarm at our appearance, but regarded us with the same frank curiosity with which we regarded him. He actually remained where he was while we diverted our line of progress to avoid him.

The birds I cannot give in detail, for I am very ignorant of birds and am only sure of the common seagull, the sparrow, and the crow. But there were parrots in a large variety, and especially numerous was one species that made a noise such as a circular saw might make while attacking a grindstone. That bird would have been of use in a ship in thick weather.

The coati-mondi was also new to us, though of course we knew of his existence. But here I must emphasise the extraordinary difference there is between animals in captivity and the same animals at large living their normal life under what I understand is called the stimulus of danger. The coati-mondi was brown-furred and snug; he lived and had his being in a perfectly fitting motor coat; he was a highly competent animal with an irritable eye. We saw only one, and he was coming head foremost down a tree — he was trotting with entire comfort perpendicularly downwards — and snuffling as though he had a cold in his head. He did not see us, for we remained standing still, and as he happened to pass us on the weather side he went by quite close and entirely preoccupied, still snuffling.

"Use yer pockerankercher!" said Wilfred; and at the sound of the strange human voice the beast jumped a foot in the air, then down again and vanished.

But the strangest thing we saw was an anteater. He looked like a mistake or the product of a dream. He did not carry a brown haystack on his back like the anteaters I have seen in captivity, but was clipped short as though from a recent hair cut. He looked powerful, and in spite of his really impossible, tubular head, he had an affable, really humorous gleam in his artificial sort of eye. He did not look either real or likely, but he was real all right.

There were also sloths and many small, rat-like creatures which, in violent contrast to the sloths, were always in a hurry. Of course we did not see all these animals at once. We saw them on different occasions, for we set out with the deliberate intention of seeing them, and sometimes I am afraid we did not know what manner of creatures we were looking at until we returned to the ship and described them to Timothy Hanks, who would usually give them a long Latin name.

But the sight of all sights we saw one day in a narrow glade, and it was a sight that still comes to me in my dreams and wakes me with its horror. It was in a narrow, natural alleyway through the thick undergrowth that fringed the lake, where we were forced to walk one behind the other. Wilfred happened to be leading, and he stopped suddenly and stepped back a foot or two in intense astonishment. We were then getting used to surprises, and at this evidence of shock in one not easily disturbed, I quite instinctively brought my repeating shotgun readily to my shoulder. Gazing over my small companion's head and down the narrow glade, my eyes encountered a five-foot pile of snake.

"Oh, my! 'Ow shockin'!" gasped Wilfred; and indeed the sight was shocking.

On the top of that living pile was the snake's head and therefore almost on a level with ours, and he looked at us with wide, unblinking green eyes, just as though he had been expecting us and was awaiting our arrival. For a moment or so sheer incredulity held us, and then, without a thought to our usual policy of non-interference, and as I happened to have the gun, I stepped in front of Wilfred. My sensations were entirely primitive and unreasoning. The snake, if you come to think of it quite logically, had as much right there as we had, but, by the same token, as he was certain to try and kill us if he could, so had we every right to try and kill him. In

other words, this was war. The impulse that
directed us — Wilfred, myself, and that preposterous monster of a snake — must have gone
back a very long way, to the ages when creatures
struggled for supremacy. No doubt we were as
detestable to the snake as the snake was to us, and
in us every fibre of our being rose up in horror at
the sight, and the death of either Wilfred, myself,
or the snake was a foregone conclusion. The
snake was looking me in the eyes, and its terrible stare was unswerving and implacable. The
markings upon its head suggested an expression
of hatred; this was accident, of course, or, at least,
perhaps it was; anyway, that expression had no
little effect upon both Wilfred and myself. We
were both, actually, terrified, nor am I ashamed
to confess it, for you must recollect that the
girth of this snake at its thickest was as great as
the circumference of a strong man's thigh. It
formed an immense pile of thick, weighty coils
that appeared, at first, to be motionless, while
the effect produced was certainly heightened by
the deep green gloom of the forest. The terror
that undoubtedly attacked us both was in every
way precisely that which affects birds and rab-
bits when under the influence of snakes of a
lesser power; but we had the God-sent reasoning
faculty of man to help us, the reasoning power
that warned us to combat this terror and

which had given us the shotgun in my hand. Therefore I waited, knowing my power to kill. Such a sight one seldom sees, for it is obviously not possible to capture the largest species of boa-constrictor such as this, and I had every intention of taking it all in. As the snake looked at me, its eyes seemed to drive at one with the same emphasis as a levelled rifle barrel, and with regard to the direction of its gaze I afterwards noted a curious fact. Wilfred maintained that the snake gazed at him unswervingly and not at me. Therefore I am not afraid to say that there must have been some hypnotic influence at work, for the snake could not have looked us both in the eyes at the same time.

The light, as I have said, was bad, so I approached a step or two entirely enthralled with the almost overpowering repulsiveness of so terrible a reptile, and the eyes of the snake never seemed to leave mine. The scales of the skin were dappled, and though I had at first thought them motionless, I discovered, with a sudden shock, that the snake was slowly unentangling itself with a smooth, gliding motion that was common to all its dreadful length. I lost no further time and raised the gun afresh, and at a comparatively short range, I aimed at the full centre of that wicked face and pulled the trigger.

The result was nothing short of terrific, and we

turned and ran some little distance, then halted and turned about, battling with a panic that was hard to resist. Again I took aim while that vast reptile thrashed the forest in its death agony with the power of a ship's propeller. Up the tunnel-like glade was that incredibly violent, twisting mass, tangling and straightening and tangling again in supreme, blind ferocity. In the midst of its horrible convulsions, which must have been only muscular activity and not the energy of life, it straightened with the quickness of a whiplash and came, with great rapidity, down the glade toward us. I gave it another shot into the pulped mass that was once its shocking head.

The snake's body stopped at the impact and contracted like a depressed spring, then, as startlingly as a released spring, it shot forward again and lay twisting slightly as dead snakes will.

"It takes a fair deal to shake me," said Wilfred, wiping the sweat off his forehead with his hand, "but I'll admit I'm shook this time! Sech things as that 'ere serpint did n't ought to be, no, they did n't! It makes a man indignant!"

We waited a long time; then we measured the snake and it was twenty-four feet seven inches in length without its head and maybe a foot of its neck, or whatever that part is called that connects the head with the rest of it. Though larger snakes have been killed in the Amazon, I do not wish to see them. Anyway, though neither Wilfred nor myself is a timid man, we discontinued, for a time, our forest wanderings.

"Ship's good enough for me," remarked Wilfred. "I'll stay aboard an' paint the galley; it needs it."

Meanwhile, trading operations continued briskly. The gold came from stream beds several days' travel to the west, and owing to the difficulties that the forest presented to a white man, and to the cheapness of the gold, we made no attempt to gather it ourselves, and were, not unnaturally, content to continue our system of barter. The Indians remained quite content with affairs and trooped off after more gold with energy and some amusement. Why we should want this more or less useless stuff they did not bother to find out, and their attitude was not unlike what the attitude of any American community would be did there arrive some extraordinary strangers willing to barter objects of practically priceless worth for some cheap and more or less easily come-by mineral deposit. Therefore I doubt if any ship's company, since the days of the infamous Sir Henry Morgan, ever earned such money as we did, for every man was to draw his share of the total according to his service rendered. And then, quite suddenly, the trading stopped.

I do not think that the gold supply had given out, but that the Indians had as many axes, knives, and so on as they wished. The Indians with whom we had been trading were only one tribe in a race, and having acquired as much property as they could carry about, they now wished to kill the trade in order that none of their friends or enemies should benefit as they had done by our unexpected arrival. This may have been childish pride, but I fancy, myself, that it was high strategy and statecraft. In vain did the captain argue and in vain did he tempt, the Indians only shook their heads politely and remained immoveable. Moreover, with equal politeness, they now desired our departure; the incident, in the words of the British Parliament, was now closed. It was tantalising, or rather would have been tantalising, had the ship not been netting an average of ten thousand dollars a day for some time; and recollecting the story about the dog with a bone, Captain Hawks accepted the inevitable, for the Blowgun Indians were, without possibility of doubt, masters of the situation — such was the power of *curare*.

So we organised a grand entertainment to round off our stay in that unforgettable country, an entertainment in which the Indians took part. It was quite a social evening, with free food, music, and fireworks. These last were some signal rockets and flares which we let off in honour of the occasion. After the Indians had sung and danced, or rather droned and hopped, an expert with the accordion from the forecastle rendered some ancient sea ditties, the crew roaring the chorus in right good style. Captain Hawks distributed a large number of presents, and the Indians presented us with four canoes and a quantity of curios; Captain Esterkay performed some conjuring tricks, to the intense amusement of the Indians and forecastle alike; Wilfred prepared a vast quantity of food, which our Indian guests ate till they could eat no more; Twocents challenged any Indian to a contest of acrobatics and beat them all to a standstill, which is saying a good deal; and I was persuaded into singing that most exquisite of all sea songs, "Tom Bowling," to the ill-concealed dismay and embarrassment of the assembled company. We had the ship gay with lights, and the scene was curious and interesting, for we were crowded and swarming with naked savages who were obviously of a fighting breed. Yet the best of humour prevailed, and we were all genuinely sorry to say good-bye. The colonel was, I know, for the Indians had done more than trade with him. They had saved his life and had refrained from eating him, and what more could any man wish! When they finally departed and were embarked in their canoes, they surrounded the ship just out of range of the lights and all together they sang some Indian chant. The effect was splendid in its dramatic quality, and after a moment of awed silence we cheered those Indians three times over at the top pitch of our lungs.

Next day there was not so much as the shadow of an Indian to be seen in the neighbourhood.

There now lay before us the difficult journey down to Para. From where we then were to Manaos was practically enemy's country, through which there was but one road, which we must take, and along which the Rio Maranon Company was bound to be waiting for us. They could wait, too, indefinitely, while time was everything to us. It was a difficult situation, and I fancy even Captain Hawks was perplexed with the future. As for our crew, they openly prayed that a downright struggle would come, and in this they were not disappointed.

According to the colonel, there was another entrance to the lake which would serve us better than the narrow river we had ascended, and though the current of this second waterway was very swift there was greater width and depth. So early next day, Captain Hawks, Captain Esterkay, the colonel, and two men went off in the launch to explore. They expected to be away all day, and meanwhile the command of the ship fell to me, and I was busy over the details of our departure. I sent Timothy Hanks off to get in a large supply of fresh meat, and with the assistance of 'Arry Ketchold I overhauled the ship. That day was full of detail both for Mr. McLushley and myself, and the time passed quickly enough. Evening came and darkness, but no sign of the explorers in the launch. Their nonappearance, however, did not disturb me, for I knew the great uncertainty that must always accompany travel in an unexplored country. The evening passed, the night advanced, midnight came and went. We mounted a bright spherical light upon the foremast to guide the wanderers, who did not show up. It was not until daylight next day that I grew uneasy, and my uneasiness turned to alarm when noon arrived without the return of the captain and his party. Then, as commander of the ship, I called an informal council of war consisting of Timothy Hanks and Mr. McLushley.

"I think," said I, "that it may be assumed that something has happened to the captain and his party. Since the colonel is one of that party, a man with wide experience of these parts, it may be also assumed that what has happened to them is no mere accident of travel. Therefore, the conclusion I have come to is that they have fallen up against some Rio Maranon force which has taken them prisoner. If, then, the Rio Maranon has got them, we must get them out."

"We must," agreed Mr. McLushley, "but we must proceed wi' due caution. The saircumstances are unusual, the deeficulties are prrodeegious, and the consequences of a mistake are awfu'!" And the Scotchman sat back with the satisfied expression of one who has made an able statement of complicated affairs.

"I am thinkin'," he continued in the same deliberate manner, "that our friends are in a poseetion that can only be tairmed extraordinair' prrecarious!" and he lit his black pipe and smoked luxuriously. "I'm also thinkin' that these Rio Maranon people will find their preesonairs most awkward cattle to handle!" and he chuckled with enjoyment. "Captain Matthew Hawks a preesonair! Eh! I'm no' envying his jailer!"

After some further discussion we decided that I should leave Timothy Hanks in command of the ship with an unofficial advisory partner in the veteran McLushley, a state of affairs only possible in such a community as ours, and that I, accompanied by Wilfred and two men, should go in search of Captain Hawks and his party; and in order that we should be able to move easily, that we should take one of the Indian canoes that had been presented to us.

The crew, when they heard of my intended departure, volunteered in a body at my request for two. But the matter was settled finally by the fact that two men, Spillings and Peabody by name, had learned to handle canoes during a temporary residence in the Canadian Northwest. Spillings and Peabody were Americans of more than ordinary effectiveness and were afraid of nothing on earth except the captain. They disclosed the possession each of a very modern revolver and plenty of ammunition, which items the laws of the ship strictly forbade them. So, when we eventually started off; what with these two delicate specimens and Wilfred (who feared no one on earth, not even Captain Hawks), and myself, we formed, I think, a small but efficient force. The crew gazed enviously down upon us, and Timothy Hanks and Mr. McLushley waved us upon our way.

I had a very good idea of the position of the channel which the captain had gone off to explore, and so directed a course diagonally across the lake, and as the afternoon was well upon its way and the sun already making westing, we paddled hard, no easy labour in such a climate. I had disposed my crew with an eye to their characters, putting Wilfred in the bow, Peabody next him, and Spillings next Peabody, while I occupied the position in command in the stern.

By the time that night descended in earnest
the prospect of learning anything definite seemed
small, but we kept along, knowing that what we
were about was the only thing to do. Imperceptibly, and without conscious effort on our part, the
canoe increased its speed. This continued for a
time before we realised that we must be in the
grip of some current. We had, by then, crossed
the narrow portion of the lake and were skirting
the shore, and it is necessary for me to emphasise
the fact that we were all of us sailors, and not
used to the navigation of rivers. Thus, in our
ignorance, we continued, satisfied with the help
that this mysterious current was affording. The
still evening lay heavy and dripping with hot
moisture in the twilight world, and grey masses
of malarial mists began to rise from the water.
Along the shore of the lake the tall trees stood
motionless, while the size of the gigantic tree-
ferns and the great twisted lianas and the tall
bunches of spear grass impressed us all with a
sense of our loneliness. Quite suddenly, the now
dimly seen forest parted and the canoe, turning
sharply, aimed for this opening with a quick
sweeping access of speed, and a Babel of startled
exclamations broke from us as we endeavoured,
too late, to gain control of our craft.

" 'Ere! Full astern!" gasped Wilfred, as we
raked the water with our paddles in desperation

and without effect, for the canoe slid onwards amazingly, and like a train entering a tunnel, shot into this natural, sluice-like canal!

Half a moment of frantic work showed us convincing proof of our helplessness, and after a short panic of energy we resigned ourselves to keeping the canoe in midstream. The water round us had an unruffled glass-like surface as it sucked downwards, and as the minutes passed it dawned upon us and our ignorance that we must be approaching a really tight fix. But I am afraid that such is the innate boyishness of sailors that we all thoroughly enjoyed the experience.

"People pay money fer this!" piped Wilfred in the bow, "at 'ome, in Hearl's Court! The Water Chute costs yer a tanner a time, and 'ere we are 'avin' all fer nothink!"

The time went by and still brought no change. Occasionally we passed through rough patches of water, but we always managed to keep our canoe in line with the current that continued to carry us onward at the rate of a motor boat. I do not now know how far we travelled, but I am certain that we went a long way, quite fifteen miles, before there came any change to alarm us. And then the water grew rougher, was heaped about in a nasty way, and roared unpleasantly in our ears. Still, as there was nothing to do but keep on, on we went, with Wilfred giving high whoops of glee in the bow. And then, as suddenly as we had entered these rapids, we as suddenly left them, and shot like an arrow over more tranquil waters, and came, finally, to rest in a wide river that was black and almost motionless in the night. We should, I think, have then realised that we had accidentally escaped drowning by a fortunate chance, had not there appeared before us a sight that swept all thoughts of the rapids from our minds.

Brilliant with many lights, a wide-beamed river boat lay apparently at anchor.

The sight was a tonic to our rather stretched nerves. Wilfred was for immediately boarding the steamer without preliminary investigation, and as both Peabody and Spillings heartily agreed, they fell to paddling briskly.

"Stop the ship," said I to Spillings, who was immediately in front of me, "or I'll lay your head open with this paddle."

So Spillings ceased work abruptly and impressed the necessity of doing the same upon Peabody, who, in turn, handed it on to Wilfred.

"You 'it me ag'in, Peabody," cried Wilfred, "an' s' 'elp me I'll beat the face orf yer the moment we git on dry mud!"

"Quit making that row!" I ordered; and for a

THE WATER GREW ROUGHER

moment or so I thought out a plan of action. Then I spoke.

"I am in command of this," said I, by way of reminder, for I knew the kind of men I was dealing with, "and what I say goes. We will drift down and have as close a look as we can, and then we may draw off again. But we may board her, but no man moves without orders from me, and my orders will be whispered. No man must make a sound, and I will do the paddling, so ship your oars."

There is no craft that can be so silently manœuvred as a canoe, and like a feather upon the surface of that slow-moving water we approached that garishly lit river steamer. At the time I wondered why she was at anchor, but I did not realise then how far we had come owing to the rapids, which had been in the nature of a short cut. In other words, as all distances in that country are measured in miles of navigable river, the steamer was some forty miles from the lake. She was of the ordinary Rio Maranon pattern, a light-draught, two-decked affair, with deck cabins and with clear spaces fore and aft for slinging hammocks. The bright light cast from many oil lamps made a close examination of her easy enough from the surrounding darkness, and like a shadow we drifted down, my paddle alone directing our course. Through an open doorway we beheld the inevitable card-players. I do not think I ever saw a Rio Maranon river boat in which there was not a group of these futile wasters of time and money. There was also the usual crowd in the bows and stern dozing and smoking, with another lot of card-players bursting into occasional shouts as their fool game proceeded. All the cabin doors were open on the lower deck, and so, with but one exception, were they upon the upper. And beside that one closed door there lounged a man with a gun. As though my eyes could see through wood I was satisfied that behind that closed door were Captain Hawks and his companions. Then with a few silent strokes of the paddle I brought the canoe round the river boat, and there, sure enough, was our motor launch moored alongside. I backed away some little distance until we could whisper in safety.

"Did you mark that closed door with the sentry?" I whispered. "Well, the Old Man and the rest are behind it. We are going to get 'em out"; and in the darkness my accustomed eyes could see a happy grin upon the faces of my companions. They looked like men who had just found a ten-dollar piece. "We are going alongside," I continued; "we shall go quickly and quietly. We will go alongside just below where that sentry stands at the closed door. I will climb aboard first, Spillings will follow, then Peabody, then Wilfred, and not all together or this pesky canoe 'll turn over. Wilfred will be the last man out, and he will not leave the ship until Peabody is clear."

"Can't I come out along o' you an' 'ave a go at the bloke with the gun?" breathed Wilfred with some irritation.

"No, you can't," said I, with emphasis. "There's a stiff proposition before us, and it's got to be handled properly — see?"

We should not be long climbing aboard, but all the same, the moment of waiting for the last man would be hard to bear and would demand character as well as courage.

"Never mind this canoe," I continued, "let her go adrift. When I get aboard I shall up-end that sentry and maybe his gun 'll go off; that 'll wake every one. So never mind where the bullet goes, but jump. If the bullet don't come my way, I 'll put the sentry out of action, and then I shall make a break for the card-players there on the upper deck a little farther along. Wilfred will come with me. Meanwhile, Spillings and Peabody will kick that door down, and the quicker they do it the better. The men on the forward main-deck we can't attend to for the moment, but they won't know how big a party we are, and I don't anticipate much trouble from them once their officers are bottled. Understand your orders? Very well, then. Come on!"

We may not have been experts in the navigation and the handling of canoes, but we came alongside that river steamer all right.

CHAPTER XIII

A RAID BY NIGHT

I GRIPPED the low rail of the lower deck and swung onto it, and reaching up I caught the upper deck and repeated the process. No one was expecting us, and no one had happened to see us come swiftly alongside. As I came up over the rail of the upper deck the sentry was in the midst of a yawn, and for a second that yawn was frozen to his face. The unfortunate man was rolling a cigarette, his rifle, with the butt to the deck, was leaning in the crook of his elbow. He was a good man that, and I felt sorry, in a way, to hurt him, but there was nothing else to be done. As time, at such moments, is measured in quarter-seconds, it was not physically possible to get his rifle up and in action before I grabbed him, and he knew it, so he turned his yawn into a most powerful yell. But the yell, though powerful, did not last. I got him by the ankles and up-ended him precisely with what you might call some swiftness, his head striking the deck where before his feet had been resting. Quick as I may have been, I hardly finished with the sentry before I noted, out of the corner of my eye, Spillings and Peabody going through the closed door. They did not kick it, they ran through it, as was manifested afterwards by the condition of their heads, and they had hard heads too. So by the time that I was running forward, Wilfred had gained my side with his gun in his hand. We raced each other and arrived at the open door of the cabin, wherein sat the men at cards, with a considerable bump, and Wilfred happening to be an inch or so in front, and being very light while I am heavy, and as our impact together in the doorway was considerable, the little cook went flying. The card-players had heard the sentry's shout of warning and our approaching steps and had risen to their feet; Wilfred, unable to stop himself from collision in the doorway with myself, arrived in their very midst with an ear-cracking whoop! Over went the card-table, the cards, the drinks, and the money, and catching one man round the neck the little Englishman and he went down together with a crack. But while this happened I shouted, "Hands up!" in a loud voice with purposeful emphasis for effect. Their hands went up, and meanwhile Wilfred bobbed to his feet again, for he hardly seemed to touch the ground. Our arrival, especially Wilfred's, must have been a shock; and then I discovered Eichholz to be among them. Strange, indeed, are the things we sometimes do without thought, for I nodded to Eichholz, and Eichholz nodded back!

All this happened, of course, in ten ticks of a watch, and then there burst forth a wild uproar from all over the ship, punctuated by some crackle of firearms and the mingled yells of Spillings and Peabody, who sounded as though they had gone mad. What precisely happened to those two gallant toughs I do not know, but the effect was as if they were having the time of their lives. Though the paid forces of the Rio Maranon Company were not human lambs, Spillings and Peabody, now gone thoroughly berserk, produced no little panic, and so far my plans had matured perfectly. While the four men in the cabin still stood with their hands aloft, I was joined by Captain Hawks, who, to my relief, now instantly took over entire command of the situation.

With prompt alacrity and while confusion reigned, Captain Hawks went amid those card-players and disarmed them all but Eichholz, whom he told to drop his hands. In this manner he acquired three revolvers which he handed to Captain Esterkay and the colonel, who arrived a moment after. The two men who had been captured with them had joined forces with Spillings and Peabody and had armed themselves with anything that came handy. And there now came a surprise for Wilfred and myself, to say nothing of those interrupted gamesters.

"Eichholz," cried the captain, "take charge of these men"; and Eichholz nodded, producing at the same time a revolver of which he had not been relieved like his companions. These last stared with blank dismay and growing rage, yet they obeyed his gesture to line up by the after bulkhead.

"Wilfred," continued the captain hurriedly, "stay here with Eichholz and help him to keep these men covered"; and Wilfred, with a gasp of astonishment, obeyed.

"Grummet and Esterkay, aft with you. Don't shoot unless you have to. Calvin and myself will go forward. We must clear this ship."

But this was easier said than done, and not by reason of the resistance raised by the Rio Maranon forces, but by our own four men who were in no mind to give up their savage fun. Had the Rio Maranon men had time to collect their forces, they would, most probably, have wiped our four men out. But panic was in charge, and they ran and scattered wildly before the ferocity of Peabody, Spillings, and their companions. Therefore it was first necessary to quell our own men into some semblance of obedience, and to my shouted orders they paid no heed. So I caught Spillings, who happened to be nearest, and seeing

red, he promptly turned his attention to myself, and absurd as it may seem, away we went,
ding-dong-dell, amid a host of our enemies!
There was no gentle hitting here; we hit for a
knock-out, and for a moment or so Spillings gave
me plenty to do. But I have not been a mate for
ten years and a second mate for longer still without practice in the rough-and-tumble order of
combat. A left-handed swing sent Spillings out;
and only then, when I had time and attention
to note it, did I hear the tumultuous sounds of
retreat.

The suddenness of the attack had more than
a little to do with our victory, and with those in
command captured and prevented from exerting
their moral influence, and with the four men
running berserk in their midst, the crew of the
river boat turned in retreat and escaped any way
they could, some actually diving into the alli-
gator-infested waters of the river. The whole
incident I do not think can have lasted more than
five minutes, and what was equally astonishing
was that so far as I know no one was killed.
Minor injuries, of course, were sustained on both
sides. The sentry I had up-ended, and who, in
consequence, had not been able to retreat with
his companions, we put with his card-playing
superiors in charge of Wilfred and Eichholz.
Spillings and Peabody, and the other two men,

were considerably knocked about; Wilfred had somehow acquired a tremendous black eye; while I discovered that I had a violently bleeding nose, though where or how I got it I do not know unless it was a present from Spillings. Captain Hawks had apparently suffered in some previous scrap, and Captain Esterkay had a torn mouth, so altogether we looked rather a hard crowd.

But we lost no time in nursing our hurts. The four men were sent down to stoke up the wood-burning furnace, while the colonel, who could do most things more or less, took charge of the engines. Eichholz, whose desertion from the ranks of the enemy was still a mystery to me, took charge of the prisoners in the cabin. Captain Esterkay took charge of the forward deck, with Wilfred to help him in slipping the cable when the colonel announced sufficient steam to move. Captain Hawks took charge in what did service for a pilot house, while I, with a rifle, stood ready in the darkness to answer promptly any rifle fire from the bank. But the men had gone without their weapons, and in total darkness we started up-stream.

"Seems to me," said the captain, a little while later, "we are not doing so badly. First it was a dog, then an Indian, then an alligator, and now a shallow-draught steamboat. But I've lost the launch, they took it with 'em when they left us

in a hurry. And I'm obliged to you, Grummet;
I was expecting you." And the captain placed a
cigar with some care between his bruised lips.

I told him of our descent of the rapids.

"Say, Grummet," he remarked when I had
finished, "I guess it's only safe at sea!"

"I guess it is, sir," I agreed.

"And then you chanced across this river boat
and just came aboard?" he asked with a grin.

"Yes, sir."

"Ah, just so."

It seemed that there were three outlets from
the lake: the one we had ascended upon arrival,
the rapids we had descended in the canoe, and
the channel which the captain had gone off to
chart. It was after the launch had descended
this third channel that the captain and his companions had come slap into the arms of the river
boat, and having been taken by surprise, and
after an exchange of a few shots, he had capit-
ulated to the inevitable, and they had been imprisoned in the deck cabin. And while they were
thus temporarily beaten, Eichholz had come to
see them, which was the first intimation the
captain had that he was aboard the river steamer.

The moon had risen over the trees upon the
port hand and afforded just enough light for
Captain Hawks to keep his newly acquired
vessel in midstream. But our draught was so

slight that we could take chances, for it was our purpose to return to the lake and to the *Martin Connor* as soon as possible. For there was an uneasy feeling in our hearts, since it had become obvious that the Rio Maranon Company had come so far afield as to penetrate to the very borders of the Blowgun Indians' country.

"Go and take a look round the ship and report," said the captain.

I found Cert'nly Wilfred in the wooden shanty that did duty as galley. He had gravitated there as a musician drifts to a piano, and he was busy with a dish of some sort for all hands. He was hilariously cheerful and bustling with a bandage over one eye and with his shirt ripped down the back. A chewed cigarette stub stuck to his lower lip and wagged about while he sang: —

> "It's a long way to Tipperary,
> It's a long way to go. . . ."

Colonel Calvin was seated watching the engines, while Spillings and company were taking turns at stoking.

"Feel all right?" I asked Spillings; "I had to hit you pretty hard."

"Yes, sir, feel all right, thank you, sir," grinned Spillings, gazing at me through one eye; "'fraid I did n't hear you speak at first, sir."

"You did n't, Spillings, but you were a bit

excited. You fight well, but you neglect your head, which I admit is hard — as hard as any I ever hit. You gave me a real live moment or two, and I have some eight-ounce gloves in the ship; we must have a go."

"Thank you, sir; I'd like nothing better."

"No ill feelin' is there, Spillings?" I asked.

"Great snakes! No, sir!"

So we shook hands.

I found Captain Esterkay sympathetically arranging a cold compress on the head of the sentry I had up-ended. I gave the latter a cigar which he instantly lighted, so I fancy he was not badly hurt.

In the cabin I found a sterner mood. Eichholz, well knowing with whom he had to deal (and who should have known better than he?), was seated at the table with a revolver in his hand. Seated in a row before him were his three erstwhile companions looking as black as a thundercloud.

"All right?" I asked him.

"Quite, thank you," he answered without withdrawing his eyes from the three men. This vigilance struck me as being a little excessive, and perhaps I felt a little sorry for those three men. They were beaten and captured, and among decent men the prisoner of war is treated more as a guest than a captive.

"Won't these gentlemen give their parole?" I asked Eichholz.

"Parole!" exclaimed Eichholz in quiet wonder. Then he shook his head with the same sad, gentle superiority of manner I had found in him from the first. "You don't know what you are talking about. You are not in the United States or Europe."

"Still," I objected, "what can they do?"

"They would give their lives to kill me, Mr. Mate," was Eichholz's reply, delivered in his lifeless, level voice.

"Oh!" said I, and grinned at him with comprehension.

Eichholz was, as the saying is, getting a little of his own back, and who knows how long a bill he had against the Rio Maranon and all its officials? It was an odd scene. Eichholz, a most remarkable man, seated at the table in an easy, lounging attitude with a large revolver cocked ready, and those three men facing him across the cabin, seated in chairs like three bad boys kept in after school. They twiddled their thumbs in irritation, or thrust their hands into their pockets and scowled, or tilted their chairs back and showed their teeth, while Eichholz talked to them in the dog-Spanish of Amazonia. I do not know what he said, but I expect it was powerful! And he seemed to have a lot to say.

I returned to Captain Hawks and reported all well; then I described to him the scene in the cabin, and he grinned.

"Eichholz's is a strange case," said he. "The older I grow the more difficult I find it to judge people adversely. Until you know a man's temperament, surrounding influences, and national weaknesses judgment is impossible. Take Eichholz. When we were prisoners in that cabin, Esterkay and Calvin feeling pretty gloomy, the door was opened and Eichholz came in. I did not know he was aboard until that moment, and when I saw him I was more than a little inclined to eat him. He began by saying that he was going to speak quickly in case the sentry outside knew a word or two of English, which was n't likely. At that I knew that we were going to get out of the mess somehow, for here was obviously a traitor in the camp of the enemy. It was, I don't mind telling you, Grummet, something of a relief, for in spite of my own private determination that this would not be my finish, I could not help seeing that we were in pretty good shape for our funerals. When innocent Americans can be shot dead without fuss a few hundred miles from American territory in Mexico, they can be shot dead without fuss 'way at the back of goodness knows where in Amazonia. I mean to say a word or two concerning our Consular Service, when I get home. Why, an Englishman, no matter where he is, if he gets into a fix, will generally find a British Consul round the corner with a battleship up his sleeve ready to help him out. No; the British know how to look after themselves and that's a fact; I guess they have made themselves so unpleasant that they have learned how; and the sooner we get a big navy and start making ourselves unpleasant when we have to, why, the better it will be for us. But I know what the folk at home will say in answer to that. They'll say that the United States is big enough and don't require any more territory, and therefore does not require a navy. I guess we'd better get a navy — a real navy that you can use in argument — or we won't keep what we've got more than a few generations, for the world's getting smaller and smaller, and Europe ain't half as dead as some politicians, who had never seen a street-car till they landed in Washington, like to make out."

The captain chewed on his cigar a moment and grunted some words beneath his breath.

"You may have been astonished to find Eichholz our friend, but you were no more astonished than I was at what he had to say. He came plump out with it too. He gave me a shorthand account of his life in this country, and though I can't repeat what he said, because it is private,

I can tell you that it shocked me, and I'm no young ladies' seminary! All that we have heard about this rubber business is true, but we have n't heard half. He said that his work was horrible, beyond endurance; that he was just crazy to get out of the country. He's been dead crazy to get out of this country for two years, Grummet. Their method is to get a man of ability, like Eichholz (he was a doctor in Hamburg with a good practice, but who got into trouble and was done for), offer him a good salary, and ship him up here. Then they have him. To hold him doubly sure he is persuaded by loneliness, by fever, by the despair at the wreck of his life, to come into line with their methods. Then if he tries to get away, they fall on him and tell him they will hang him for the atrocities they have forced him to commit to get rubber. The result is that he's all in pieces."

I nodded, while a casual remark of Wilfred's that, "This 'ere Earoles seems to find 'is-self 'orrible to contemplate," struck me as being singularly apt.

"So Eichholz came to me, a prisoner, and asked me to get him out of the country! The apparent foolishness of the request showed me that he was in earnest. He asked me if I would give him a passage in the *Martin Connor* if he helped us out of the fix we were then in. You can guess my answer! Some particular jackasses would think, I know, that the desire to escape was my only motive, but it was n't Grummet. I wanted to get out of the fix, of course, and I was n't half-dead either. The future looked black, but I have seen it look blacker, and I have seen the future change remarkably when you kick and keep right on kicking. No, I was more pleased than I can describe to think that I could help that man; for when all is said and done it is about all there is to the business of life, to help when you can and help in the right way. And there is plenty of help for the young and promising, and for the old and past praying for, all fixed up pretty in institutions and printed books, with slathers of money from the State and the charitable though lazy-minded. Here was a man with a past as black as your hat that he had fallen and been forced into. Of course you can say that you, or I, or, say, Wilfred, would n't have been forced. Quite so, I agree; but because one man can swim a swollen river, it's no argument that another can. No, I sort of got it into my fool head that there was more than just a commercial chance that had brought me to this country in a full-powered steamer! I was absolutely sure, then, that we should get out of that fix, but just how we were going to do so I did not know. Nor had Eichholz any very definite plan to offer, and as it might look suspicious if he stayed too long with us, he went away and promised to return later. Of course, I knew that you would make a pretty good try to help us, but we might have been delayed anyway, so that you would not be likely to start out and look for us until we were more than halfway back to Maloca. And this blame hooker pulled up with engine trouble and we anchored where you found us while they tinkered her up. By the time they had finished, it was night and apparently they decided to wait for daylight before continuing. Then I heard that sentry let off a yell, and the thud of his head hitting the deck sounded familiar. "That's Grummet arriving," I thought, and next moment Spillings and Peabody came through the door. Oh, I guess it was all intended, like most things, only it was left to us to make either a good job or a bad one according to how much there is in us!"

When, after ascending what we had come to call the Western Passage, we hove in sight of the *Martin Connor* in the early hours of the following day, our appearance — an obvious Rio Maranon river boat — caused some excitement. As we approached I saw Timothy Hanks and Mr. McLushley with glasses to their eyes. Then suddenly, Timothy, that most undemonstrative young man, lifted his hat and yelled. We replied by prolonged blasts upon our whistle. As we came wallowing alongside the crew shouted hilariously, and when you come to think of it our return was rather triumphant. Even Mr. McLushley grinned almost amiably at us and exchanged a short nod with the captain.

"Ye'r back, I see, Captain Matthew Hawks," said he.

"I am, Mr. McLushley," answered the captain, "and I traded the launch for this river boat."

"Oh, ah! Just a wee trip for your health, was it, combining pleasure wi' business, maybe?"

"Just that, and a little exercise."

"Oh, ah! I note that ye seem to have run into something wi' ye'r face, Captain Hawks."

"Yes. I think I remember brushing against something." And the two men laughed quietly, while their eyes shone as they looked at each other, and in them was the light of affection that mocks the spoken word.

"There'll be some sick men doon the river?"

"Sick at heart. I have four prisoners with me."

"Eh! Let me have 'em in the stoke-hold to shovel coal — it's a grra-and occupation in this climate."

"No, I guess they have had enough."

"Na. Nathin''s enough for yon."

Captain Hawks smiled. "The Scotch," said he, "are a great race, but they are not forgiving."

We brought our prisoners aboard, and the captain talked to them and explained that we should drop them in one of the ship's boats as we passed Maloca if they would behave themselves meanwhile. If they gave this undertaking they might have free run of the ship and every consideration as passengers. With this they naturally agreed. We then took the river boat a little way off and anchored her with an insulting letter to the Rio Maranon Rubber Company tacked up in her pilot house, and there, for all I know, she remains to this day.

There is, in the voyage of a ship, a dramatic quality not often equalled in other commercial ventures. When the *Martin Connor* hove up her hook and started homeward there was not a man aboard her that did not feel, in varying degrees according to his powers of perception, this dramatic quality of which I speak. There was no chanty to be raised as an outlet for emotions, the very modern and efficient steam capstan did its work, and once more the ship began to vibrate to the pulse of the smooth-running engines.

We negotiated the Western Passage in a manner startling to the oldest sailor aboard, for the swift-running stream became almost rapids in places owing to the corkscrew current, and to shoot rapids in an ocean-going ship is a matter to lift one's hair from its roots.

The Rio Maranon Company was ready for us, first, at Maloca, where the crew of the river boat had long since arrived. The captain had arranged to pass Maloca at daybreak, intending to rush the situation. But there must have been some one on the lookout for us, while the moment or two taken in dropping our prisoners in a boat (we left them the boat) gave time for every one in Maloca to come forth with rifles, and we fled past in a rain of bullets that rang and clattered about the iron ship while we crouched in shelter. Captain Hawks, from inside the iron charthouse, blew blasts upon the whistle in answer, and Wilfred, at great risk to himself, crawled across the deck and, opening one of the swing-scuppers an inch or two, replied with very accurate rifle fire, for I was watching with the glasses through another scupper in the stern. In little over four minutes we were gone by, but it was a fine, lively moment or two.

At nights, when we anchored, we patrolled the river round the ship with a boat and returned to sea conditions, standing watches throughout the twenty-four hours. At this work we had one or two alarms, but the intruders always turned out to be river Indians desirous of selling fish! And as the days and nights passed in vigilant uneventfulness a spirit of unrest crept through the ship. Was n't the mighty Rio Maranon Company going to put up some kind of fight at all? As for the captain and myself, this calm was very grateful. To be quite truthful, we wanted to get out of that country, and if there was no fighting the sooner should we escape. However, this apparent inaction on the part of the enemy was suspicious and we never relaxed one moment of watchfulness. The days and nights followed, and once in the main Amazon stream we were often able to steam at full speed through most of the night or as long as the moon lasted.

"I don't understand it!" said the captain, puzzled and uneasy; "there must be something coming, but I wish I knew what it was!"

As for the crew they were openly contemptuous and disappointed, while Wilfred would spit eloquently whenever he happened to mention the name of the Rio Maranon Rubber Company, and it would be hard to be ruder than that.

But the days went on and the nights went on, and in this anticlimax we all, I think, in our different ways, suffered various forms of "nerves"; for to be momentarily expecting an attack that does not come is one of the most difficult trials to bear. With the river current to help us our mileage per twenty-four hours down-stream was a very different matter from our distances run while steaming up. We passed Manaos before Manaos had time to grasp the fact, and no hint was made of stopping us. And then, one day, we passed a Liverpool steamer inward-bound. We regarded her with hungry intensity, for, to us, after what we had been through, her efficient and seagoing appearance was strangely affecting. She blew us a salute upon her whistle, and her Old Man upon his bridge exchanged a wave with Captain Hawks. Oh, it was fine to see white men again, and to come in touch with the sane, clean, organised world once more! That Liverpool steamer, with her white awnings and paintwork and her shining brass, was a sample of all we had left and all we were returning to. It was like meeting a decent individual in a dangerous city slum! Then the forest resumed its preponderance in the landscape and we continued on and on, awaiting, ready, some obscure attack that never came.

It is difficult for me to describe how sick we had all become of that evil country, of the colour and smell of the water, of the unending wall of trees, of the ever-present dripping heat, of the wholly damnable insects. But the thought of home, of the healthy, wind-swept open sea kept our spirits up. I now do not wonder at men becoming worse than savages after years in such a place.

Every ounce of which the ship was capable was

pressed out of her by Mr. McLushley without
an undue consumption of coal. Even his iron
and leather constitution had not improved and
though he said nothing in particular he was as
anxious to leave those forests and rotting jungles
and fevers as any of us.

We were now, practically speaking, out of the
Rio Maranon Company's country, though we
kept a bright lookout for trouble. But no further trouble awaited us, which worried us not
a little, until we arrived at Para, where surprises
came thick and fast.

To begin with, we found that Mr. Alonzo
Makepeace Massingbird had been a naturalised
citizen of the United States; and the international difficulties concerning his death fell from
the problem beneath the capable hands of the
American Consul at Para. He had everything in
readiness for us, with legal assistance; and after
a sweating, steaming morning and afternoon the
incident was closed with a reprimand and a dinner. But that was not the only surprise.

The Rio Maranon Rubber Company had gone
into liquidation!

This was due to a sudden depression following
upon an inflated boom in rubber, the organised
competition offered by the Malay States and
Ceylon, the manipulation of rubber markets by
a European ring, the impossibly high freights

demanded both upon the upper river and for oversea transport, the excessively high cost of living and therefore of production in the upper Amazon country, and last, but not least, to the general shocking mismanagement and devilish habits of the Rio Maranon rubber collectors.

At the news of the practical death of the Rio Maranon Company, a most extraordinary change came over the face of Eichholz! He altered, literally, in a moment. His tragic mask fell from him; it was almost uncanny and profoundly moving. With his freedom there had come another man, and since the Rio Maranon was now non-existent, so far as its power to injure him was concerned, he bade us good-bye at Para, intending to wait a little and grow more used to a less extra-tropical climate before leaving that part of South America altogether. So he passed out of our lives, a strange, interesting, and attractive man, horribly punished for his sins, yet picking up his life and continuing with fortitude and fine spirit.

CHAPTER XIV

It was early upon a fine, merrily tempestuous morning, with a strong breeze blowing steady and warm, that the vast muddy prospect of the estuary gave place to the clean blue ocean before the bows of the *Martin Connor*. Across the great arch of the sky were hurrying clusters of brilliant clouds, and the fresh salt wind rippled the tightly stretched awnings. An hilarious spirit prevailed, and when, at first imperceptibly, the ship began to lift to the great Atlantic seas after being so long in the stagnant stillness of the Amazon, there was a cheer in every heart aboard her. The ship herself seemed to catch the mood, and she rolled and pitched like a living thing set free, and oh, the pleasure of those swinging decks — to feel the ship once more a ship at sea, with the strong salt air humming in the scanty wire rigging! And the cleansing purity of the sea and the lofty, wind-borne flights of spray seemed to wash us, as though with antiseptics, of all the horrors, the fevers, and the wickedness of that great and sinister river.

Only two members of the ship's company were unhappy at the movement. They were Maryjane, the Indian, and Percy, Wilfred's alligator. Maryjane had been deeply offended at the suggestion that we should leave him at Para where the American Consul had promised to find him a job. So there was nothing else to do but take him with us, though after a few hours in the open Atlantic Maryjane would have willingly been back in his native swamps. However, seasickness did him no harm, and he is now, I understand, following the useful and placid occupation of ship-keeper in Galveston. Percy, the alligator, was somewhat discommoded with the salt water. But his cage on the after main-deck was as dry as anywhere, and we built around him a shelter of blankets and canvas. He is now, and doubtless always will be, a possession of the city of New York, where he occupies the distinctive position of being the largest alligator in captivity. He is, by the by, a crocodile and not an alligator, though just in what the difference consists I do not know, though I expect Timothy Hanks knows and understands!

Stadger, dumbfounded at the moving decks and the occasional swilling of the seas through the clanging scuppers, barked himself into semi-hysteria with sharp staccato barks that went through your head like a knife, until Wilfred, exasperated, fell to hammering his hard muscular body with his fists.

On the voyage home Timothy Hanks completed a work he had been engaged upon which
he entitled "Notes upon the River Amazon," a
compilation of facts and figures as unenlightened
and as correct as an invoice; the publication of
which, in a scientific journal, brought him fame
in a quiet way.

Captain Hawks, from the latest figures obtainable in Para, computed that we had over two
and three quarters millions of dollars' worth of
gold on board at a conservative estimate.

"Not bad, for a single cruise, Grummet," said
he with a grin.

"No, sir, not bad."

We were in the charthouse, the doors hooked
back to the clean sea wind. Captain Alexander
Esterkay, feeling cold, filled one end of the settee;
Colonel Ezra Calvin, long, loose-jointed, and
angular, sat in the other, two very typical specimens of North and South. Twocents, in obedience to a call, arrived with a muffler and a greatcoat from Captain Esterkay's cabin. The boy's
appearance was greatly changed from the day he
had given chase to the captain's hat upon the
wharf at Galveston. He was not much fatter, it
is true, for he was of a slim habit of body. The
change was in his expression and in his bearing.
A boy still, but a boy for whom the world had its
place, and for whom the world held a future. His

reclamation was complete. There was nothing of the street-bred urchin left; he was a responsible, reputable member of society. Captain Esterkay gave him two years at a technical college, then back he went to sea, and he is now, so I have just heard, third mate in a good line of fruit steamers running between Cuba and New York. Some day he will doubtless have his own command.

"Two an' three quarter million!" repeated Captain Esterkay in a mild surprise; "say, Matthew, that's all — all right, is n't it?"

"It is, Alexander, for all of us," replied the captain, putting away his papers in the chart-house desk.

I stepped out onto the bridge-deck into the warm wind and sunshine. The horizon was complete, a sharply defined ring enclosing the bright, foam-patched, flashing sea. 'Arry Ketch-old, ponderous and slow, moved about amid the watch that was busily painting. Mr. Andrew Kinnaird McLushley sat in an oil-stained deck-chair with spectacles on his nose, deep in the poetry of Mrs. Hemans.

As I climbed the ladder to the bridge the happy chant of the engines came up through the sky-lights, and to their rhythmical measure Cert'nly Wilfred in the galley raised his voice in song.

THE END

The Riverside Press

CAMBRIDGE . MASSACHUSETTS

U . S . A